YEADON'S REGISTER

of

L N E R

LOCOMOTIVES

Volume Twenty-Two

Class B1 (B18), B2 (B19), and B3 to B9
The Great Central 4-6-0's

YEADON'S REGISTER OF L.N.E.R. LOCOMOTIVES - VOLUME 22

EDITOR'S NOTE & ACKNOWLEDGEMENTS

Welcome to Volume twenty-two of *Yeadon's Register of LNER Locomotives.* Herein are the former Great Central Railway 4-6-0 tender engines of LNER Classes B1 to B9. It was originally planned to include the GCR 4-4-0 tender engines also in this volume but space considerations regarding the photographic coverage, even with 128 pages available, meant that the D5 to D12 classes will feature in their own volume at a later date.

The nine classes featured in this volume were all built to the designs of one man - J. G. Robinson. Arguably none of the GCR 4-6-0 classes could be regarded as being amongst his best designs; any accolades as such would surely go to his D9, D10, D11 and O4 classes. However, the erstwhile 4-6-0's certainly had the Robinson stamp on them and handsome engines they were. Though some of the classes were intended for express passenger work and others for mixed traffic duties, it was in the latter employment that these engines actually ended up, their express passenger duties being short lived for one reason or another.

That most of them lasted to the very end of the LNER period and even into early BR days says more for the motive power shortage of the Second World War period than their fairly long lives might suggest. Their eventual demise was hastened by the droves of Thompson B1's being delivered to the LNER at the end of the Company's existence. None were preserved.

So, with this volume, the *Register* sees the type B letter designated engines finished with, hopefully with a flourish.

It goes without saying that Eric Fry has once again contributed so much to this volume not just checking the proofs but adding much in the way of missing information or clearing up some of the uncertainties that are generated in a work such as this.

Victoria and Oliver at the University of Hull Archive Department continue to put up with our endless requests, not to mention the toing and froing - just put it down to experience - thanks. Thanks also to Mike and Mick; those level crossings need sorting out!! And another thanks to the lads at Amadeus for their continuing professionalism in turning out the finished product.

Annie, Jean and Simon, though seemingly in the background, are thanked for the support and kind words given as each volume is completed.

Finally, thanks to you the reader. We appreciate your support too.

The next Register, Volume 23, will feature the balance of the Q classes - those 0-8-0's of the former North Eastern, and Hull & Barnsley railways - Q5 to Q7 and Q10.

The Yeadon Collection is available for inspection and anyone who wishes to inspect it should contact:-
The Archivist
Brynmor Jones Library
University of Hull
Hull
HU6 7RX
Tel: 01482-465265
A catalogue of the Yeadon collection is available.

First published in the United Kingdom by
BOOKLAW/RAILBUS 2001 in association with CHALLENGER
382 Carlton Hill, Nottingham, NG4 1JA.
Printed and bound by The Amadeus Press, Cleckheaton, West Yorkshire.

INTRODUCTION

This volume covers the nine classes of Great Central 4-6-0 tender engines which became LNER Classes B1 to B9. All the engines were built to the designs of J.G.Robinson and though perhaps they were not amongst the most successful of his numerous designs, they certainly looked impressive and graceful too in most cases.

Standardisation was one of the important points with these nine classes. For instance the B1 and B4's were basically to the same design except for the size of driving wheel therefore most parts were interchangeable. The B2, B3, B7 and B8's shared the same boiler type; likewise the B5 and B9 latterly shared the same boilers as the Q4 0-8-0's, the cylinders of the Q4 could also be fitted to the B5 whilst the B6's along with the O5 2-8-0's also used the same boiler type. Needless to say boiler mountings and other parts were also interchangeable. The tenders basically, were all, save for minor detail differences, of the 4000 gallon type built to a design that was shared amongst other Robinson classes including the D9, D10, D11, J11, O4 and O5's.

It was probably this 'standardisation' which prolonged the lives of many of the 4-6-0's. However, towards the end of the LNER a new Standard design of 4-6-0, the Thompson B1 was being brought into traffic in ever increasing numbers as replacement for these and the various Atlantic classes.

One of the striking aspects of the GC 4-6-0 was that several of the classes had been built for the specific and most important haulage of express fish trains from Grimsby to all parts of the GC system. It probably seems inconceivable today that locomotives were specially built to haul the vast quantities of fresh fish then consumed by the nation. That traffic is no longer in being nor are the fishing fleets that brought home the 'catch'.

Withdrawal of the ex-GC 4-6-0's had begun in 1939 with one each of classes B4, B5 and B9, but the start of the War resulted in the reinstatement of two of them and there were few further withdrawals until mass delivery of the new Thompson B1's began during 1946. Thereafter the GC engines were rapidly eliminated, the last class to become extinct being Class B7 in 1950.

Alas none were preserved but at least two examples of Robinson's distinctive designs have survived, both sharing the honour of being his most successful engines, one built for passenger service, the other to haul goods.

B1

The two members of LNER Class B1 (GC Class 8C) were built by Beyer, Peacock at their Gorton foundry in December 1903 (No.195) and January 1904 (No.196). Regarded as experimental, they had 6ft 9in. coupled wheels and two 19in. x 26in. outside cylinders (No.195 came out new with 19½in. cylinders but these were later changed) and were primarily intended to haul passenger trains between Manchester and London. Two similar engines, Nos.192 and 194, but with the 4-4-2 wheel arrangement were built by Beyer, Peacock at the same time and it was this type that was multiplied, becoming LNER Class C4.

Neither was superheated when new but in August 1912 No.195, was ex Gorton with a superheated boiler and new 21in.

cylinders with piston valves. This boiler was second-hand, taken from Class B4 and equipped with a 24-element superheater. However, in September 1920 it reverted to a saturated boiler and had two more general repairs before getting a new superheated boiler with 22 elements in March 1926. No.196 had to wait until LNER days before it got a superheated boiler on 9th April 1927 when, at the same time, it came out with piston valves and 21in. cylinders.

In 1906 another ten engines to the same design but with 3in. smaller coupled wheels, intended for fast goods and fish traffic, were delivered from Beyer, Peacock. These ten were classified 8F on the GCR (LNER B4) and are dealt with latter.

No.5196 was ex Gorton in December 1936 with a heating connection fitted to its front end. No.5195 was never so fitted.

Both engines were used during the mid-1920's by the Bridge Stress committee. On the 22nd November 1924 No.5195, along with C4 Atlantic No.5360, was at Cambridge in connection with bridge testing. Whilst sixteen months later, in March 1926, No.5196 was fitted at Doncaster with a speed indicator and associated gear for use by the Bridge Stress committee.

In order to give up the premier B classification to Thompson's new 4-6-0's, the twins were reclassified B18 from April 1943.

After a career which saw both engines working the length and breadth of the former GC lines, they ended their working days at Annesley shed both going there on the 21st September 1947 from Colwick. During the LNER period they had virtually spent most of their lives together. 5195 spent an unbroken fourteen years at Woodford from 1926 until moving to Colwick in 1940, however, 5196 had a three week stint at Neasden in April 1928 so spoiling its same length of time at Woodford.

No.195 changed to 5195 in July 1924 but No.196 had the C suffix from November 1923 until it became 5196 in April 1925. Both survived to get their 1946 numbers and were numbered 1479 (October) and 1480 (September) respectively.

Both engines were withdrawn on the last day of the LNER having survived for twenty-five years as one of the Company's smallest inherited classes.

B2

Six engines comprised this class designated Class 1 (LNER Class B2) on the GCR. All were built at Gorton, the first No.423, coming out in December 1912.

The most striking change from the previous GC 4-6-0's was the lack of outside cylinders, however, the two inside cylinders were 21½in. in diameter with a 26in. stroke. The 5ft 6in. boiler was superheated, the first of the Robinson 4-6-0's to be so built. This pattern of boiler was also used on classes B8 and the later B3 and B7, but went through three distinct phases of development. Those fitted at first to Class B2 and the first engine (No.4) of B8 had a 24-element superheater and 157 small tubes. These seven boilers proved to be unsatisfactory and on the remaining ten engines of Class B8 a change was made whereby the diameter of the elements was reduced and the number of small tubes went down to 139. All these boilers rotated only among the engines of classes B2 and B8, including two spares put in service in 1917.

In 1918 two more replacement boilers were built and put on class B2 Nos.426 and 428. In these the number of superheater elements was increased from 24 to 28 and the number of small tubes reduced further to 116. This pattern of boiler became standard for B2 and B8, also the new engines of B3 and B7 design.

The very large diameter inside cylinders were also a problem on Class B2 and as early as April 1921 No.427 had them lined up to 20in diameter. Nos.423 and 424 were similarly altered in 1922, and No.5426 in 1938. Meanwhile No.5423 had acquired a new set of 21½in. cylinders in 1937. The LNER alloted class parts B2/1 (21½in.) and B2/2 (20in.) to these variants. Orders were given in 1943 to line all the engines up to 20in. but there is no record that this was actually done.

During the following three months of 1913 four more Class 1's came out from Gorton but the final engine of the class did not emerge until December. All the engines were named from the start, No.423 after the General Manager and the others, Nos.424 to 428, after cities into which the GCR ran trains. The LNER removed the name CITY OF LONDON from No.5427 in September 1937, when it was required for the streamlined B17 engine No.2870.

Although intended to haul the principal expresses between Manchester and London, these engines were soon taken off those duties in favour of the D10 'Directors' because of steaming and axle problems. All were at first allocated to Gorton for the London jobs but three were transferred to Immingham during WW1 whilst the three remaining at Gorton were put onto fast goods trains to and from the Capital.

After the conflict they amassed at Gorton and were again tried on the London expresses but were soon relieved of these turns by the more reliable D11 'Directors', after which they were put on secondary passenger and fast goods workings, which as events turned out was to be their lot until withdrawal. In 1924, No.5428 went to Ardsley for a couple of months and No.5423 went to Neasden for six weeks after which all six settled down for the next twenty years at the sheds situated on the northern section of the former GCR. Gorton, Sheffield and Immingham sheds had the most use out of the B2's though during WW2 both Langwith Jct and Lincoln sheds had a couple each. Eventually they all settled at Immingham from where they were all withdrawn. During their time at Immingham, besides being used on all sorts of duties, the B2's would regularly visit King's Cross in the mid-1930's on specials from Grimsby organised by a local travel agent.

Three engines came out in GC green livery whilst the other three appeared in goods black (a premonition perhaps?) but the black liveried engines soon gained passenger green and then managed to keep the green until into WW2 which, considering their secondary role since well before Grouping, must be something of a record. Ironic too when other more capable engines which took over their intended duties in WW1 should be given black livery during the 1920's. Nos.425, 426, 427 and 428 got the C suffix to their numbers in 1923, the others going straight to their 5XXX numbers. In the 1943 scheme the numbers 1472 to 1477 were allocated but this was changed in 1946 when the then remaining four engines in the class became 1490 to 1493.

In August 1945 the B2's were reclassified B19 to give the B2 classification to Thompson's rebuilt B17's.

No.5426 was the first of the class to be withdrawn - during the War, in December 1944 - followed by No.5424 a year later. The other four lasted until 1947.

B3

The first engine of Great Central Class 9P, No.1169, was built at Gorton in November 1917. Another five 9P's were built but not until the second half of 1920. Classified B3 by the LNER, these massive 4-cylinder engines were to be the largest passenger engines employed by the GCR.

All carried names from new but two lost them, No.6167 LLOYD GEORGE shortly after Grouping and No.6166 EARL HAIG in October 1943 when it was rebuilt by Thompson.

The four cylinder arrangement was adopted to alleviate the problems encountered on the B2 class engines where the inside cylinder design put too much of a strain on the driving axleboxes. The four cylinder design allowed the strain to be divided with the inside cylinders driving the leading axle and the outside cylinders driving the middle axle.

The engines were superheated from new and were equipped with piston valves. 12-feed Intensifore lubrication was fitted to all the class from new except for No.6165 which was fitted with an 18-feed Intensifore system when it emerged from Gorton in July 1920.

Gresley snifting valves replaced the original Robinson combined circulating and blower valve and header discharge valve after Grouping. Whilst Detroit or Eureka type lubricators replaced the Intensifore systems.

In an effort to cut down the excessive coal consumption of these engines the LNER rebuilt Nos.6166 and 6168 with Caprotti valve gear in 1929. Later, in 1938 and 1939 respectively, Nos.6167 and 6164 were similarly rebuilt. These four were reclassified B3/2 whilst the original engines became B3/1.

No.6166 was subject to another rebuilding in 1943, this time by Thompson and when it emerged from shops it was for all intent and purposes a B1 except that it kept its original 6ft 9in. driving wheels. This engine became Part 3 of B3 class.

The Thompson rebuilding was not carried out to any more of the class and though it was deemed to have been a less than successful rebuild due no doubt to the persistent frame fractures, No.6166 was the last of the class to be withdrawn.

No.1169 had Reliostop automatic train control fitted from new but this was removed 6th October 1919, no other members of the class were so fitted.

The engines were divided between Gorton and Immingham when new with the former shed's engines being used on the less important expresses to Marylebone. Shortly after Grouping Nos.1165, 1166, 1167 and 1169 were tried out on the GN main line between King's Cross and Leeds and in the following year all the class were working between London and Leeds. In 1927 both Copley Hill and King's Cross sheds got rid of their B3's back to Gorton, their use on the ECML having been deemed to be less than successful.

Back at Gorton, two of the class were transferred to Neasden later in the year to balance the workings of the important express between Manchester and London (Marylebone); some of the 'Directors' previously used on these trains being sent to Copley as replacements for the B3's on the Harrogate Pullman trains.

The B3's did not last long on the London expresses and during the 1930's the Gorton ones shuffled between that shed and Sheffield Neepsend whereas the two at Neasden enjoyed regular employment on trains to Leicester and back, right up to the end of WW2 except for a short period in 1934/35 when B17's replaced them temporarily.

B1. No.196 still with its original 19in. diameter cylinders and slide valves, as built in January 1904, was running as such to its March/April 1922 repair when the footsteps between the leading and middle coupled wheels were removed. Marylebone station, 9th June 1919.

B2. No.423, built December 1912 at Gorton and here fitted with an indicator shelter for testing, was the first of a class of six built to haul main line express passenger trains but they were quickly out-performed by the 'Director' class engines on the London extension and they then worked on the secondary expresses between Manchester and Cleethorpes.

B3. One engine, No.1169, was built in November 1917. Originally it had Ramsbottom 4-column safety valves but two Ross 'pops' replaced them in 1919. In April 1922 the Robinson combined circulating valve and blower was taken off but the header discharge valve was retained. Gorton shed.

B4. At Grouping all ten engines, Nos.1095 to 1104, were still as built, with 19in. cylinders, slide valves and using saturated steam. Minor alterations were removal of the piston tail rods, and addition of plating to the outside of the originally open tender coal rails. One of the two whistles had also been discarded.

B5. Six engines, Nos.1067 to 1072, were built by Neilson and Co. in 1902. No.1067 as at Grouping, still has its original tender with open coal rails. Nos.1069 and 1070 had acquired tenders ex J11 class with solid coping by Grouping (*see* photo 17 page XX). Woodford shed, August 1923.

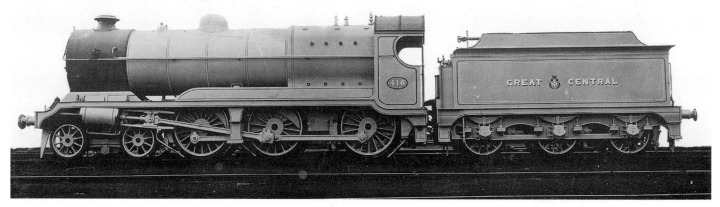

B6. One engine, No.416, was built in 1918 being the fifth of a batch of ten, the other nine being 2-8-0's which became Class O5. Top feed, Intensifore lubricator, header discharge valve, also combined steam circulating and blower valve were all Robinson features to be fitted.

Immingham was another shed which benefited from the GN enginemens dislike of the B3's and in 1927 again received engines of the class. They kept the engines on the same duties and like Neasden got some good results from them. At the beginning of 1939, Immingham and Neasden sheds shared the class equally between themselves both having established a regular work pattern for the class.

At the start of war Immingham lost its trio to Woodford who used them on the West of England trains between Banbury and Sheffield. Neasden in the meantime continued to use their three on express passenger work though by now the loads of such trains had become increasingly heavier and the B3's, along with the Gresley Pacifics now allocated to Neasden, shared this heavy work. Two of the Woodford engines went to Copley Hill in 1942 for use between Doncaster and Leeds. Occasionally these engines would venture further south to Grantham on what can only be described as the very heavy trains of the period.

Gorton got the Copley Hill engines back later in 1942 and the one from Woodford joined this pair to work the Manchester to London expresses again in the absence of the Pacifics which had returned to the GN main line.

Towards the end of the war and in the immediate post-war years the class was shared at various times by Immingham, Neasden and then Lincoln and before withdrawal they all ended up working in England's second largest county.

Like other ex-GC 4-6-0's, the B3's were subject to a second renumbering in 1946, their first choices Nos.1480 to 1485 were never used and the second choice, Nos.1494 to 1499 was only applied to the first five engines, No.6168 being withdrawn before it had 1499 applied. The B2/3 rebuild, No.1497 (ex-6166) was numbered in the BR scheme and this was the only member to survive into BR use.

The first withdrawal was No.6168 in September 1946 and four more went in the latter months of 1947 whilst the sole survivor 61497 lasted until April 1949.

B4

Ten engines comprised Class B4 (GCR Class 8F), all delivered by Beyer, Peacock in 1906. Numbered 1095 to 1104, these engines had saturated boilers throughout their GC careers but were superheated by the LNER.

Their 6ft 7in. coupled wheels gave them the appearance of passenger engines but they were in fact designed for express goods and fish trains. Originally the wheels were 6ft 6in. diameter before the fitting of thicker tyres.

When superheated in the mid-1920's, three of the class were fitted with 21in. cylinders and piston valves when they received a superheated boiler. Three more got 21in. cylinders and piston valves at a later date whilst the remaining four kept their 19in. cylinders with slide valves. This change in cylinder size and type of valves created sub divisions within the class and in December 1928, by which time all had been superheated, those with larger cylinders and piston valves became B4/1 and those with original equipment were B4/2. Originally the sub-divisions B4/1 and B4/2 applied to those that were saturated and superheated respectively, no account being taken of the type of cylinders. Class parts B4/3 and B4/4 were created in 1935 applying to former B4/1 and B4/2 cut down to the 13ft load gauge.

These ten engines shared the same pattern of boiler as the two Class B1's that had been built 2½ years earlier. Two spares were constructed in 1909 to permit rotation, then in 1912

boiler No.1213 (off Class B4 1103) was converted from saturated to superheated for trial and was fitted to B1 No.195. No others were altered and further replacement saturated boilers were produced from 1919 to 1924. It was then decided that both classes should be given superheated boilers. During the period 1925-28 thirteen such boilers for the twelve engines were provided - ten new ones and three conversions from the youngest saturated boilers. Subsequently only four more superheated boilers were made, the last in 1933.

The 1939-45 war kept B1 and B4 in service longer than anticipated. In 1946/47 recourse was made to converting two spare boilers from Class O4 to the B4 type. The essential alteration was to make the firebox less deep. The boilers concerned were: 3395 New on O4 No.5417 in May 1940. Converted and fitted to B4 No.6103 (later 1488) in September 1946. It returned to use on Class O4 in December 1949 (No.63779). Boiler No.3265 was new on O4 No.5382 in October 1936. Converted and fitted to B4 No.1482 (ex 6097) in March 1947. Cut up with the engine in November 1950.

Though painted GC passenger green when new, this class acquired black paint with red lining before Grouping but the LNER restored the green livery and this continued until the middle years of the war when unlined black became the norm. However, the sole named example in the class, No.1482 (ex 6097) IMMINGHAM, regained green livery in March 1947 and kept it through to withdrawal.

Gorton, Grimsby and Neasden sheds shared this class for work on express goods and fish trains, the latter shed also employed them on express passenger trains as far as Leicester for which duty they were quite capable. During the Great War the Neasden engines transferred to Mexborough and that shed used the B4's on troop trains amongst other important traffic. By Grouping all the class were resident at Neepsend shed from where they worked to all corners of the former GC system.

March had the use of the four of the class in 1923 but their height restricted them operationally and within a few months they returned to Sheffield and Mexborough. Some then went to Doncaster for working fish traffic, New England also had four in 1925 which they used on goods trains to London. In the meantime No.6100 had gone to Copley Hill in November 1924 to star what was to be a long association between the B4's and the West Riding.

Within a year all the class were allocated to either Ardsley or Copley Hill sheds and they were used mainly on King's Cross expresses between Leeds and Doncaster. Sometimes these duties took them down to Grantham. Excursion work saw them used right through to King's Cross in the 1930's and they were regular visitors to the resorts on the east coast.

March shed again played host to three of them in 1933 and this time they did a lot of passenger work both north and south of March even though they had not been cut down to comply with the LNER composite gauge. The March B4's moved to Lincoln in 1935 where they were employed on further important passenger work. Immingham had a couple during 1937 and these engines found their way to London on special workings. In 1939 half the class were at Copley Hill, four at Lincoln and No.6103 was at Retford but besides these sheds, Ardsley, Bradford and Langwith Junction had use for them during the war years and they could be found working goods and express passenger trains.

They ended their lives working from Ardsley and Lincoln and were finally ousted from those sheds by the growing numbers of Thompson B1's.

Under the LNER renumbering scheme, which was drawn up in 1943, B4 class were to become 1490 to 1499. When the scheme was implemented this had changed and the surviving nine engines took the numbers 1481 to 1489 between August 1946 and January 1947. Nos.1482, 1483, 1485 and 1488 all survived into BR days but none received 60000 series numbers.

The first withdrawal was in July 1939 but No.6095 was reinstated because of the war situation. However, this engine turned out to be the first withdrawal after all when it was condemned in 1944 after suffering heavy damage in a collision at Woodhead. The others lasted until 1947 at least when five of the class were condemned. One went in 1948, two in 1949 and the last one, No.1482 IMMINGHAM became the sole example of Great Central 4-6-0 before it was condemned in November 1950 and then cut up at Gorton..

B5

The GCR Class 8 was Robinson's first 4-6-0 design for the Company and, at the time of their introduction, were the largest engines the company possessed. A total of fourteen engines eventually comprised this class, all built by outside contractors.

The first six engines, Nos.1067 to 1072, were supplied by Neilson & Co. in November 1902 all with saturated boilers. They were designed to haul express fish trains and for that role they were fitted with 6ft 0in. driving wheels (later changed to 6ft 1in. with new tyres). Their initial allocation was Grimsby and Neasden and because of their work they gained the nickname "Fish engines".

Another batch of eight engines came out from Beyer, Peacock in the early months of 1904 and these too had 4ft 9in. saturated boilers. The cylinders of the Class 8 engines were interchangeable with the 8A 0-8-0 goods engine (LNER Q4) though the 4-6-0 had to have a shallower firebox to accommodate the higher position of the coupled axles.

In the first year of Grouping moves were made to superheat this class and in the June of that year No.184 was fitted with a 5ft 0in. boiler (Diagram 15) used by the O4 class engines. The firebox was one foot longer than the normal Class B5 boiler. Piston valves and 21in cylinders were also fitted but not until August 1924. Because this boiler had a deeper firebox it was necessary to pitch it some 9½in. higher than was normal. Necessarily the boiler mountings were altered also which changed the engines appearance somewhat. To finish off, a double side window cab was fitted. No other members of the class had this drastic treatment though nonetheless it had a pleasing appearance. Instead, the superheated version of the Q4 boiler (Diagram 17) was chosen to be fitted to the B5's and this was carried out between 1926 and 1936. Even No.5184 got one of the smaller diameter superheated boilers in 1927 so bringing it in line with the others. At that time it lost the double side window cab and reverted to the normal cab with cut-outs.

The use of the Q4 superheated type boiler on class B5 necessitated a 7in. increase in the pitch due to the deeper firebox, resulting in shorter boiler mountings which affected the appearance considerably. Before receiving this type of boiler, two B5's ran with saturated Q4 boilers. these were No.5183 (June 1929 to May 1933) and No.6070 (January 1934 to April 1936).

Six more engines were fitted with 21in cylinders and 10in. piston valves during the late 1920's and 1930's but none had mechanical lubrication of any sort. Sight feed lubrication sufficed throughout.

At the time when No.5184 carried the 5ft 0in. boiler it was designated Class B5/2 whilst the rest of the class became B5/1. As the smaller superheated boiler was fitted to the class another sub class appeared for those engines so fitted - B5/3 - but once all the class got the same treatment the sub divisions were dropped in 1937.

As mentioned above, the first six engines went to Grimsby and Neasden sheds to work the express fish trains. Of the eight in the second batch Gorton received its share also. Besides their usual express fish train work, Neasden shed used them for express passenger work at least as far as Leicester. By Grouping Mexborough had seven B5's whilst the others were divided between Gorton and Immingham. Mexborough used these engines on fish traffic besides goods and excursion work.

Ardsley shed got four just after Grouping, No.6067 ex Mexborough along with Nos.5183, 5184 and 5185 all ex Immingham, but these were exchanged for B4's in 1924. Mexborough then lost its B5's to Doncaster. Lincoln had eight of the class by 1931 and these were used for all sorts of work including station pilot at Lincoln (Central). Immingham, Lincoln, Sheffield and Woodford hosted the class in varying numbers up to wartime but by 1943 they were concentrated at Mexborough and the new shed at Sheffield Darnall working passenger and goods trains, the former mainly to Hull.

In 1946 the three Darnall engines moved to Trafford Park for passenger work on the CLC. Their stay west of the Pennines was short and within the year all three had moved to Mexborough where the rest of the class had now congregated. By now they were run down and they worked out their last days on banking duties between Wath and Dunford Bridge besides having charge of the occasional goods train.

In the original 1946 renumbering these engines were to be 1300 to 1312, one engine having been withdrawn in 1939. Only two engines carried the first numbers, Nos.5186 and 5187 becoming 1311 and 1312 for a few months in early 1946 but new numbers were issued from 1678 to 1690 and they all carried these.

The first withdrawal was No.6070 in March 1939 but no others succumbed until 1947 when six went for scrap. Four more went in 1948 and two in 1949. The lone survivor, No.1686 lasted until June 1950 on banking duties from Mexborough shed, one of the last GC 4-6-0's to be withdrawn.

B6

The first engine of this class (GCR 8N No.416) was built at Gorton in July 1918 but the other two (Nos.52 and 53) did not appear until March and April 1921 respectively. The engine number 416 had originally been planned as being part of a batch of ten 8M 2-8-0's (LNER Class O5) being built but instead it came out as a 4-6-0 and was virtually identical to the 2-8-0's except for the wheel arrangement.

The two outside cylinders carried by this class were introduced to overcome the driving axlebox weaknesses encountered with the earlier inside cylinder B8's (Class 1A) and essentially they worked. The coupled wheels were 5ft 8in. diameter. This class gained a good reputation for free steaming and running.

The last two engines (Nos.52 and 53) came out with double side window cabs complete with a rearward extension to the roof whereas No.416 had the early type of cut away cab with no such extension. All three kept their original cab configuration with no change throughout their lives.

The boilers of the B6 engines were interchangeable with the O5's and this was often done at shopping. However, as the O5's were gradually being rebuilt to O4's the number of boilers available for interchange was dwindling and two new Diagram 15B boilers had to be built in 1941 for the B6 engines to enable them to be kept in traffic during the war.

All three were fitted with Robinson 4-feed Intensifore lubrication from new but during the mid-1930's this was removed in favour of Wakefield type mechanical lubrication.

None of the class were ever fitted with ash ejectors, the only GC 4-6-0's never to have them. Only one of the class (No.5052) ended up with twin handles for the smokebox fastening, the other two retaining the wheel and handle fastening.

Though all had the standard GCR 4,000 gallon tender, No.5416 had one with Iracier axleboxes until 1932.

No.416 stayed at Gorton until 1919 when it went to Neasden. The other two, when new in 1921 went to Woodford, and were joined there by No.416. Their work at Woodford was mainly hauling the West of England trains between Sheffield and Banbury until those duties were taken over by new B7's. All three were at Gorton by Grouping but then one by one, starting with No.5416 in September 1925, they moved to Sheffield (Neepsend) shed. In February 1928 they moved on to Ardsley for a six year period of working from the ex-GNR West Riding sheds including Copley Hill and Bradford.

In mid-1934 the B6's returned to Sheffield from where they worked right through the war years until moving again to Ardsley during July and August 1946. This turned out to be their final allocation and all were withdrawn at the end of 1947, No.1346 (5416) in November, with the other two being condemned on the last day of the LNER.

The three B6's were allotted numbers 1328 to 1330 in the 1943 scheme but in 1946 when the scheme was implemented this was changed and they became Nos.1346 to 1348. Their 1947 withdrawal then freed these numbers for latter use by Thompson's B1's which were still to be delivered.

B7

This, the largest class of GC 4-6-0, Class 9Q (LNER B7) first appeared in May 1921, Gorton turning out Nos.72, 73 and 78 in May , June and July. Vulcan Foundry built ten more in the latter months of 1921, these being numbered 36, 37, 38 and 458 to 464. In the twelve month period from August 1921 to August 1922, Gorton added another ten to the fleet, Nos.465 to 474. Before the last ones of that Gorton batch came out, next door neighbour Beyer, Peacock & Co. delivered five more of the class, Nos.31 to 35. Finally, during 1923 and 1924 Gorton built another ten B7's, Nos.475 to 482, 5483 and 5484, bringing the total to thirty-eight.

Designed for mixed traffic duties, the B7 with its 5ft 8in. coupled wheels was a smaller wheeled version of the B3 passenger engines. It had the same four cylinder layout, boiler and frame although the coupled wheelbase was slightly less allowing improvements to be made to the valve gear and to the ashpan at the rear end.

Those ten engines which came out after Grouping conformed to the LNER composite load gauge with reduced cab and boiler mountings height and these were classified B7/2 whilst the GC built engines became B7/1.

Intended to take the place of all the other GC 4-6-0's, the B7's went to all parts of the system where their forebears worked. Immingham, Leicester, Neasden, Sheffield, Woodford

and of course Gorton all had them in varying numbers, the latter shed having the lion's share. Throughout the LNER period this remained largely the case except the couple that were based at Leicester went to Annesley early on in 1924. Brunswick shed at Liverpool got No.5031 in 1938 and that stayed there until 1943 working the 7.0 p.m. goods to Sheffield. The Woodford engines, besides being used on the more usual fast goods turns, would sometimes work coal trains to London. By 1941 Woodford shed had by far the largest allocation of B7's with seventeen based there.

The B7's could be found on excursion work too, their fast running being most useful. Immingham engines worked also into King's Cross on the specials originating from Grimsby.

By 1943 the B7's had all congregated at Gorton and from that shed they worked just about every job; from there they would also be loaned to Heaton Mersey, Trafford Park and Brunswick when required. Though Sheffield had a small number of B7's up to the war, it had nothing like the eighteen which went there for a two year spell in 1945.

During the post-war years they could also be seen once again on various jobs in the London area but they remained concentrated in the Manchester and Sheffield areas until finally being displaced by Thompson B1's.

Besides getting the 5000 addition to their numbers after Grouping, the whole class got their 1946 numbers too but only eleven got BR numbers, all in 1949, which were the second lot allocated to them. The first BR numbers, 61360 to 61397, were required for the Thompson B1's which were still building but two of the class, 61391 and 61396 managed to get theirs applied before the second 617XX number range was allotted.

The B7's were regarded as Robinson's best 4-6-0 even though they burnt large quantities of coal but they could easily perform either on fast goods turns or passenger duties.

This was the only GC 4-6-0 class to remain intact at Nationalisation however, in just over two years after Vesting day the whole class had been withdrawn, No.61711 (ex 61391) being the last and outliving the others by at least five months

B8

LNER Class B8 consisted of eleven engines built by the GCR at Gorton. The first to appear, No.4 was built in June 1913 but the other ten (Nos.439 to 446, 279 and 280) were built between the period July 1914 to January 1915. Classified 1A by the GC, with 5ft 7in. coupled wheels, these were a smaller wheeled version of Class B2 (GCR Class 1) and four of them were named.

Designed to haul express goods and fish trains, the class was at first divided between Gorton, Immingham and Neasden. That these engines were ever built considering the problems encountered with the Class 1 engines, is a mystery.

In an effort to make them more efficient engines, two of the class (5004 and 5443) got 20in. cylinders fitted as replacements for the original 21½in. type but 5443 reverted to the larger type in 1935. No.5004 meanwhile kept the smaller diameter pair to withdrawal and from 1938 was classified B8/2, the rest being B8/1's.

Ross 'pop' safety valves replaced the original four column Ramsbottom type between 1920 and 1926.

Three of the class were fitted for oil burning in 1921 and although two of those reverted to coal burning later in the year the third engine, No.445, kept it until December 1923 although for some of that period it had also been fitted to burn a coal/oil mixture (colloidal) of fuel.

B7. Three engines, Nos.72, 73 and 78, were built at Gorton between May and July 1921 of which only No.72 was temporarily fitted for oil firing. Top feed, combined steam circulating and blower valve, header discharge valve, Ross 'pop' safety valves, and Intensifore sight feed lubricator were standard features of the design.

Besides their designed use on express goods, they also undertook stopping passenger and excursion work. From 1920 their work was being taken over from Neasden and Immingham by the new B7 (GCR 9Q) 4-6-0's and they went to various sheds, including Leicester and March before settling at Annesley and Colwick. From the latter shed they performed on fitted goods trains to Manchester Deansgate and to Hull. Annesley used the B8's on coal trains to Woodford and at weekends they were often to be seen on Nottingham area excursion work to the East Coast to the resorts both north and south of the Humber. London was another destination for them on pre-war weekends. They had two short spells at March but their height restricted their operating area from that shed. In fact the class never did qualify for the LNER composite load gauge which is probably one of the reasons why they spent most of their lives working over the former GC lines.

In 1943 the whole class ended up at Annesley shed but in 1947 after withdrawals had started the remaining nine moved to Darnall, their last move, and from where the class slowly contracted in numbers.

Allocated numbers 1331 to 1341 in the initial 1946 scheme (but not taken up), they had to be renumbered again to 1349 to 1359 to make way for further Thompson B1's. All got the second of the 1946 numbers but none gained a BR number even though five were allotted them.

The first withdrawals started in March 1947 (1359) and five more were condemned during that last year of the LNER. Three went in 1948 and miraculously two lasted until early 1949 when the last one No.1357 was withdrawn in April and LNER Class B8 became extinct.

B9

The GCR Class 8G (LNER B9) was another attempt by Robinson to mate a passenger engine body with mixed traffic engine wheels this time 5ft 4in. diameter. Built by Beyer, Peacock in 1906, these ten (Nos.1105 to 1114) engines also had outside cylinders similar to the B4's to which they were then related.

At first no spare boiler was provided to allow rotation. To permit this to happen, in April 1910 No.1112 was fitted with boiler No.827 taken from Class B5 No.182. This boiler, although of the same length, was 4ft 9in. diameter instead of the normal 5ft 0in. on Class B9. It was retained by No.1112 until November 1918 when it returned to use on Class B5.

(opposite, middle) B8. One engine, No.4, was built in 1913 as a small wheeled version of Class B2, and was unchanged as at Grouping. It was named GLENALMOND. Note that there was no snifting valve on the frame at the base of the smokebox.

(opposite, bottom) B9. Ten engines, Nos.1105 to 1114, were built in 1906 by Beyer, Peacock, without superheaters. At Grouping they were still without superheaters. Note the ash ejector supply pipe to the rear of smokebox on the left side. March shed, May 1924.

Evidently this caused a crisis amongst the B9's because No.1112 remained out of service for nearly a year awaiting a replacement boiler, whilst No.1107 was not available for even longer, April 1918 to August 1919, for the same reason. Replacement boilers to the original designs were at last constructed from 1919 onwards. However, in 1924 it was decided to adapt the Class Q4 boiler with superheater for use on that class and also B9, and a little later B5. It became known as No.9 Standard at Gorton, and took the Diagram 17 classification on the LNER. The diameter was 4ft 9in. and it had the deeper firebox of the Q4 class type, so that on Class B9 it had to be pitched 4in. higher than the original.

Superheating was introduced from 1924 but this was not completed until 1929 and during the interim period those superheated engines became B9/2 whilst the saturated engine were B9/1's. The first engine to be superheated, No.6109 was fitted with 21in. cylinders at the same time but although this enhanced its performance no other B9's were so fitted.

The GC divided the class between Gorton and Lincoln sheds for working fast goods trains. No.1114 was allocated to Mexborough for a short time after delivery but it was actually shedded at Bradford GN shed to work a night good train to Manchester.

At Grouping, although generally losing most of their fast goods duties to the B6 and B7's, the B9's remained at both Gorton and Lincoln sheds but in 1925 Gorton hosted them all until 1927 when Trafford Park started an association with the B9's which was to last virtually throughout their lives. In that year four engines went to Trafford Park and that number remained virtually constant throughout to the war years. They had two main duties at that shed, the evening Deansgate goods which was worked as far as Colwick and the Ardsley goods another overnight working. Gorton shed used them on two other important goods trains originating in Manchester, the nightly Ardwick to Lincoln and the overnight Ardwick to Marylebone.

Weekends saw the B9's utilised on excursion trains but they also performed on regular trains such as the Sunday morning Manchester to Cleethorpes stopper which was a Gorton lodging turn.

During the early years of the war Heaton Mersey shed acquired No.6111 which had actually been withdrawn in 1939 but was reinstated after overhaul to help out in the war effort. Ironically this engine was the last of the class to survive. When 6111 returned to Gorton in 1941 it was replaced by two more B9's at Heaton Mersey one of which worked the Liverpool portion of the ex Marylebone Down Mail from Godley Junction and returned with the morning goods from Halewood to Dewsnap. The other engine of the Heaton Mersey pair worked coal empties to Penistone and returned with a full load to Stockport.

From 1945 to withdrawal they worked mainly in the Cheshire Lines area doing all kinds of work except haulage of the fastest passenger trains.

This was another class which was allocated 1946 numbers only to have them changed for higher numbers (1342 to 1351 then changed to 1469 to 1478). All managed to carry the second number. Only four engines survived into British Railways ownership, the others being withdrawn in the latter months of 1947. Of those four only two wore the BR numbers allotted to them, 61469 and 61475.

The last B9 to go was 61475 (ex-6111) in May 1949 and that, like many of the other GC 4-6-0's, was cut up at Dukinfield.

No.195, which was built in December 1903, had been rebuilt in August 1912 with 21in. diameter cylinders and piston valves, and with superheater, although it reverted to saturated steam from March 1926. It then retained the 21in. p.v. cylinders and its sight feed lubrication, but lost the footsteps. It is seen here as L.&N.E.R. 195 but still with GCR cab numberplate, ex works on 20th January 1923 but not ex paint shop until 14th April 1923. It changed to 5195 from 26th July 1924. Doncaster.

In November 1923 No.196 got LNER green livery as No.196c and was fitted with this new, but still saturated boiler, which had a shorter dome and also a rectangular cover around the Ramsbottom safety valves. The smokebox also had ash ejector fitted. It became No.5196 from 18th April 1925. Nottingham Victoria.

CLASS B 1 (B 18 from April 1943)

5195

Beyer, Peacock 4541.

To traffic 12/1903.

REPAIRS:
Gor. 27/4—17/8/12.**G.**
*Superheated boiler, piston
valves and 21in. cylinders fitted.*
Gor. 14/8—18/9/20.**G.**
Saturated boiler fitted.
Gor. 26/8/22—20/1/23.**G.**
Gor. 24/5—26/7/24.**G.**
Gor. 5/12/25—6/3/26.**G.**
Superheated boiler fitted.
Gor. 10/12/27—4/2/28.**G.**
Gor. 21/12/29—25/1/30.**G.**
Gor. 19/9—31/10/31.**G.**
Gor. 21/10—18/11/33.**G.**
Gor. 23/3—13/4/35.**G.**
Gor. 17/10—7/11/36.**G.**
Gor. 1—29/4/39.**G.**
Gor. 22/3—26/4/41.**G.**
Gor. 12—30/10/43.**G.**
Gor. 25/5—8/6/46.**G.**
Gor. 31/12/47. *Not repaired.*

BOILERS:
835.
1213 (*exB4 6103*) 17/8/12.
1205 (*exB4 6100*) 18/9/20.
833 (*exB4 6102*) 20/1/23.
681 (*new*) 6/3/26.
55 (*ex spare*) 25/1/30.
122 (*exB4 6101*) 31/10/31.
798 (*ex5196*) 18/11/33.
802 (*exB4 6100*) 7/11/36.
798 (*ex5196*) 29/4/39.
681 (*exB4 6096*) 26/4/41.
798 (*ex5196*) 30/10/43.
121 (*ex5196*) 8/6/46.

SHEDS:
Gorton.
Immingham 27/4/23.
Woodford 28/4/26.
Colwick 3/3/40.
Leicester 5/4/43.
Colwick 4/7/43.
Leicester 16/1/44.
Neasden 20/10/46.
Colwick 26/6/47.
Annesley 21/9/47.

RENUMBERED:
5195 26/7/24.
1479 20/10/46.

CONDEMNED: 31/12/47.
Cut up at Dukinfield 3/48.

5196

Beyer, Peacock 4542.

To traffic 1/1904.

REPAIRS:
Gor. 21/10—11/12/09.**G.**
Gor. 19/1—7/12/18.**G.**
Gor. 11/3—29/4/22.**G.**
Gor. 22/9—10/11/23.**G.**
Gor. 14/2—18/4/25.**G.**
Don. 2—6/3/26.**N/C.**
*Speed indicator and gear fitted
for use by Bridge Stress
Committee.*
Gor. 8/1—9/4/27.**G.**
*New superheated boiler, piston
valves and 21in. cylinders fitted.*
Gor. 15/12/28—2/2/29.**G.**
Gor. 18/10—22/11/30.**G.**
Gor. 31/10—5/12/31.**G.**
Gor. 29/7—19/8/33.**G.**
Gor. 12/1—2/2/35.**G.**
Gor. 5—26/12/36.**G.**
*Heater connection fitted at front
end.*
Gor. 4—25/2/39.**G.**
Gor. 5/4—3/5/41.**G.**
Gor. 18/8—4/9/43.**H.**
Gor. 1—29/12/45.**G.**
Gor. 31/12/47. *Not repaired.*

BOILERS:
836.
1206 (*exB4 6096*) 11/12/09.
1210 (*ex spare*) 7/12/18.
122 (*new*) 10/11/23.
797 (*new*) 9/4/27.
128 (*new*) 22/11/30.
798 (*exB4 6102*) 5/12/31.
797 (*exB4 6103*) 19/8/33.
122 (*ex spare*) 2/2/35.
798 (*ex5195*) 26/12/36.
922 (*ex spare*) 25/2/39.
798 (*ex5195*) 3/5/41.
121 (*exB4 6102*) 4/9/43.
128 (*exB4 6098*) 29/12/45.

SHEDS:
Immingham.
Woodford 27/4/26.
Neasden 31/3/28.
Woodford 23/4/28.
Colwick 3/3/40.
Leicester 26/5/40.
Colwick 5/5/46.
Neasden 20/10/46.
Colwick 26/6/47.
Annesley 21/9/47.

RENUMBERED:
196c 10/11/23.
5196 18/4/25.
1480 29/9/46.

CONDEMNED: 31/12/47.
Cut up at Dukinfield 3/48.

In March 1926, No.5195 was fitted with a new superheated boiler which had a Gresley anti-vacuum valve and Ross 'pop' safety valves. A new 'plant pot' chimney was fitted, but it kept the sight feed lubrication, and neither engine was fitted with Robinson's Intensifore or any other mechanical lubricator. The number was moved from the tender to cab side from 25th January 1930 but No.5195 retained the brass beading to its rear coupled wheel splashers and the whistle was still mounted on the cab roof.

In November 1936, No.5195 regained a GC style chimney although this was 4¾in. shorter than its original GC chimney. The whistle was also moved from the cab roof to a position between the safety valves and cab front. Neither engine was ever fitted with hinged glass sight screens on the cab sides. Skelton Junction, 1939.

No.5196 was rebuilt in April 1927 with 21in. diameter cylinders, piston valves and superheater. Its new boiler had Ross 'pop' safety valves and a Gresley anti-vacuum valve was fitted, as was a 'plant pot' chimney.

In November 1930, the number was moved from the tender to cab side but this engine had the splasher beadings removed, allowing more space to display the number.

Although repaired only a month earlier than the other engine, in November 1936, No.5195 did not have a heater connection fitted at the front end, nor was it ever so equipped. Ex works on 26th December 1936, No.5196 had a heater connection fitted (see following page, bottom). Woodford shed, July 1937.

Until they were shopped in April (5195) and May (5196) 1941, both engines retained fully lined green passenger livery. This was all the more surprising when the corresponding 4-4-2 engines had to make do with black painting from 1928 and on the GCR as also on the LNER, they were classed - and used - as mixed traffic engines.

In 1943 both lost the LNER on their tenders and got the wartime NE, No.5195 in October and 5196 in September. They survived to get LNER again during 1946 and No.5196 got a distinctly lower dome. Note that its tender retained water pick-up apparatus. Darnall shed, September 1946.

At its last repair No.5195 (1479 from 20th October 1946) in June 1946 got a very angular dome cover and it also changed from wheel to a second handle for its smokebox door fastening, but its upper lamp iron remained on top of the smokebox. It did however lose its ash ejector but managed to keep its brass beadings to the splashers. Neasden shed, April 1947.

(*right*) No.5196 became 1480 on 29th September 1946 and at its last repair from which it was ex works on 29th December 1945, it kept ash ejector, wheel on smokebox door, and the lamp iron on top of the smokebox. Dukinfield works, February 1948.

(*below*) Both engines were withdrawn on the LNER's final day, 31st December 1947, and they were hauled from Gorton to the carriage works yard at Dukinfield where they were broken up in March 1948. The tenders, which had been attached to them since at latest June 1920, went back to Gorton for other service but were cut up there at the end of June 1948. Note that No.1480 retained the operating hand wheel for the water pick-up gear on the tender. Dukinfield works, March 1948.

When new in 1912/13, three B2's Nos.423, 425 and 428 were in passenger green, but the other three Nos.424, 426 and 427 were in the goods livery of black with red lining. Only Nos.423 and 428 were named from new. During June 1913 the other four were named and all six were in green livery by Grouping. Manchester (Central) loco yard.

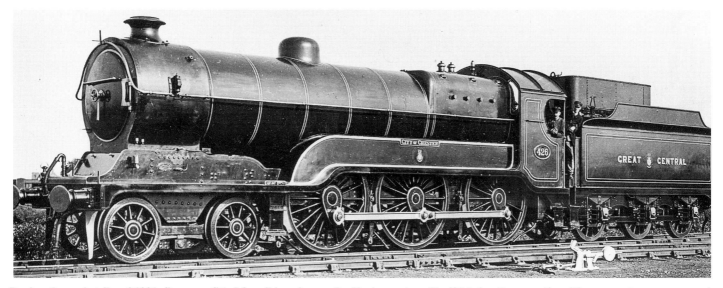

During the coal strike of 1921, five were fitted for oil burning on the Unolco system, No.425 being the exception. The apparatus was removed in September/October 1921 but was then stored for potential later use.

From October 1919 to sometime in 1921, the tender of No.423 was equipped for the Reliostop system of mechanical automatic train control. The apparatus had been removed completely from No.423 before Grouping.

CLASS B 2 (B 19 from August 1945)

5423

SIR SAM FAY

Gorton.

To traffic 12/1912.

REPAIRS:
Gor. 7/7—18/8/17.**G.**
6 feed Intensifore fitted.
Reliostop fitted 14/10/19, no
date for removal.
Gor. 26/8—28/10/22
Ross 'pops' fitted.
Gor. 31/5—26/7/24.**G.**
Gor. 19/12/25—20/3/26.**G.**
Gor. 24/7/26.**N/C.**
Converted to oil burning.
Gor. 15/1—26/3/27.**G.**
Converted to coal burning.
Gor. 17/9—15/10/27.**L.**
Gor. 10/3—5/5/28.**G.**
Gor. 27/7—14/9/29.**G.**
Gor. 27/9—15/11/30.**G.**
Gor. 2—30/4/32.**G.**
Gor. 25/2—8/4/33.**G.**
After collision at Loughborough
31/1/33.
Gor. 8—29/12/34.**G.**
Gor. 16/1—20/2/37.**G.**
New cylinders.
Gor. 10—31/12/38.**G.**
Gor. 23/11—21/12/40.**G.**
Gor. 17/3—3/4/43.**G.**
Gor. 25—28/8/43.**L.**
Gor. 24/3—5/5/45.**G.**
Gor. 19/4/47. *Not repaired.*

BOILERS:
1545.
1698 *(new)* 18/8/17.
1848 *(exB3 6167)* 28/10/22.
1849 *(exB3 6167)* 26/7/24.
1848 *(ex5425)* 20/3/26.
  77 *(exB7 5465)* 5/5/28.
 424 *(exB7 5038)* 30/4/32.
1922 *(exB7 5464)* 29/12/34.
3007 *(exB7 5476)* 31/12/38.
3017 *(exB3 6164)* 21/12/40.
 571 *(ex5427)* 3/4/43.
3046 *(new)* 5/5/45.

SHEDS:
Gorton.
Neasden 25/9/24.
Gorton 12/11/24.
Sheffield 27/1/30.
Gorton 16/9/30.
Sheffield 9/12/30.

Immingham 27/6/33.
Sheffield 21/11/42.
Immingham 5/5/45.

RENUMBERED:
5423 26/7/24.
1490 8/12/46.

CONDEMNED: 19/4/47.
Cut up at Gorton.

5424

CITY OF LINCOLN

Gorton.

To traffic 1/1913.

REPAIRS:
Gor. 9/3—25/9/18.**G.**
Gor. 17/1—6/3/20.**G.**
Ash ejector fitted.
Gor. 11/3—27/5/22.**G.**
New 21½in. cylinders..
Bushed 8/8/22 to 20in.
Ross pops fitted.
Gor. 8/12/23—1/3/24.**G.**
Gor. 9/1—27/3/26.**G.**
Gor. 31/7/26.**L.**
Converted to oil burning.
Gor. 15/1—26/3/27.**G.**
Converted to coal burning
Gor. 21/4—16/6/28.**G.**
Gor. 23/3—27/4/29.**G.**
Gor. 25/10—6/12/30.**G.**
Gor. 2/7—6/8/32.**G.**
Gor. 14/10—11/11/33.**G.**
Gor. 9/6—7/7/34.**L.**
Gor. 20/10—17/11/34.**G.**
Gor. 2—30/5/36.**G.**
Gor. 11/12/37—8/1/38.**G.**
Gor. 20/1—24/2/40.**G.**
Gor. 11/5—8/6/40.**L.**
After collision.
Gor. 16/10—28/11/42.**G.**
Gor. 22/4—20/544.**G.**
Gor. 1/12/45. *Not repaired.*

BOILERS:
1546.
1549 *(ex5427)* 25/9/18.
1546 *(ex spare)* 6/3/20.
 388 *(new)* 1/3/24.
  6 *(new)* 6/12/30.
 579 *(exB7 5469)* 11/11/33.
 784 *(exB7 5470)* 30/5/36.
1845 *(exB7 5480)* 8/1/38.
3031 *(new)* 24/2/40.
3005 *(exB7 5461)* 20/5/44.

SHEDS:
Gorton.
Sheffield 17/8/31.
Gorton 7/6/33.
Lincoln 11/10/36.
Immingham 13/12/42.

RENUMBERED:
5424 1/3/24.

CONDEMNED: 1/12/45.
Cut up at Gorton.

5425

CITY OF MANCHESTER

Gorton.

To traffic 2/1913.

REPAIRS:
Gor. 28/6—26/7/19.**G.**
Gor. 28/5—2/7/21.**G.**
Ross 'pops' fitted.
Gor. 25/11/22—27/1/23.**G.**
Gor. 21/6—16/8/24.**G.**
Gor. 31/10/25—6/2/26.**G.**
Gor. 2/7—20/8/27.**G.**
Gor. 23/2—13/4/29.**G.**
Gor. 10/1—14/2/31.**G.**
Gor. 2/7—6/8/32.**G.**
Gor. 14/4—12/5/34.**G.**
Gor. 1/2—21/3/36.**G.**
Gor. 8/5—12/6/37.**G.**
Gor. 15/10—19/11/38.**G.**
Gor. 11/11—16/12/39.**L.**
Gor. 28/9—9/11/40.**G**
New cylinders.
Gor. 17/12/42—13/2/43.**G.**
Gor. 16/12/44—17/2/45.**G.**
Gor. 4/7/47. *Not repaired.*

BOILERS:
1547.
1548 *(ex5426)* 26/7/19.
1547 *(ex spare)* 2/7/21.
1848 *(ex5423)* 16/8/24.
1698 *(ex5427)* 6/2/26.
1744 *(ex5428)* 20/8/27.
1934 *(exB7 5034)* 14/2/31.
1845 *(exB7 5468)* 12/5/34.
3008 *(new)* 21/3/36.
 539 *(exB8 5446)* 13/2/43.

SHEDS:
Gorton.
Immingham 10/6/33.
Sheffield 22/2/35.
Immingham 24/7/39.

Langwith Jct. 28/5/42.
Immingham 19/6/42.

RENUMBERED:
425c *by* 6/6/24.
5425 16/8/24.
1491 22/12/46.

CONDEMNED: 4/7/47.
Cut up at Gorton.

5426

CITY OF CHESTER

Gorton.

To traffic 3/1913.

REPAIRS:
Gor. 26/1—22/6/18.**G.**
Gor. 22/1—19/3/21.**G.**
Ross 'pops' fitted.
Gor. 10/2—21/4/23.**G.**
Gor. 17/1—21/3/25.**G.**
Gor. 7/8/26.**L.**
Converted to oil burning.
Gor. 4/12/26—5/3/27.**G.**
Converted to coal burning.
Gor. 30/6—13/10/28.**G.**
Gor. 22/3—24/5/30.**G.**
Gor. 17/10—28/11/31.**G.**
Gor. 12/11—3/12/32.**G.**
Gor. 17/3—21/4/34.**G.**
Gor. 7—28/12/35.**G.**
Gor. 19/6—17/7/37.**G.**
Gor. 25/6—13/8/38.**G.**
New cylinders.
Gor. 8/4—13/5/39.**H.**
Gor. 29/3—3/5/41.**G.**
Gor. 8—29/5/43.**H.**

BOILERS:
1548.
1744 *(new)* 22/6/18.
 424 *(new)* 21/4/23.
1926 *(exB7 5460)* 13/10/28.
1928 *(exB7 5034)* 3/12/32.
 274 *(exB3 6166)* 21/4/34.
1934 *(exB7 5036)* 28/12/35.
3032 *(new)* 3/5/41.
3023 *(exB7 5474)* 29/5/43.

SHEDS:
Gorton.
Sheffield 9/9/30.
Immingham 4/5/33.
Sheffield 27/2/35.
Immingham 20/739.
Langwith Jct. 29/5/42.

5426 continued.
Immingham 28/6/42.
Sheffield 21/11/42.
Immingham 13/12/42.

RENUMBERED:
426c *after 21/4/23 at shed.*
5426 21/3/25.

CONDEMNED: 22/12/44.
Into Gor. for cut up 30/12/44.

5427

CITY OF LONDON
(name removed 9/37)

Gorton.

To traffic 3/1913.

REPAIRS:
Gor. 22/12/17—13/4/18.**G**.
Gor. 4/12/20—26/2/21.**G**.
Steam sanding & Ross 'pops fitted.
Gor. 22/4/21.**L**.
Cylinders bushed to 20in.
Gor. 23/9—18/11/22.**G**.
Gor. 3/1—7/3/25.**G**.
Gor. 12/6—28/8/26.**G**.
Gor. 26/11—4/2/28.**G**.
Gor. 2/3—20/4/29.**G**.
Gor. 18/10—22/11/30.**G**.
Gor. 12/3—9/4/32.**G**.
Gor. 12/11/32—7/1/33.**G**.
Gor. 5/8—23/9/33.**G**.
Gor. 19/1—2/3/35.**G**.
Gor. 29/2—21/3/36.**G**.
Gor. 13/3—17/4/37.**G**.

Gor. 19/3/38.**L**.
Gor. 2—30/7/38.**G**.
Gor. 24/8—12/10/40.**G**.
Gor. 30/12/42—6/2/43.**G**.
Gor. 22/7—26/8/44.**G**.
Gor. 2/11—14/12/46.**G**.

BOILERS:
1549.
1550 *(exB8 5004)* 13/4/18.
1698 *(ex5423)* 18/11/22.
1547 *(ex5425)* 7/3/25.
303 *(exB8 5440)* 28/8/26.
610 *(exB3 6164)* 22/11/30.
8 *(exB3 6166)* 9/4/32.
599 *(exB8 5444)* 23/9/33.
3001 *(new)* 2/3/35.
576 *(exB7 5478)* 21/3/36.
3023 *(new)* 30/7/38.
571 *(exB8 5004)* 12/10/40.
3036 *(new)* 6/2/43.
3021 *(exB7 5468)* 26/8/44.
3002 *(exB7 5468)* 14/12/46.

SHEDS:
Gorton.
Immingham 25/4/28.
Gorton 15/12/28.
Sheffield 24/11/29.
Gorton 24/11/30.
Sheffield 2/5/33.
Gorton 26/6/33.
Lincoln 22/6/39.
Immingham 21/11/42.

RENUMBERED:
427c *by 4/9/24.*
5427 7/3/25.
1492 19/8/46.

CONDEMNED: 14/11/47.
Into Gor. for cut up 15/11/47 but sent to Dukinfield works for breaking up.

5428

CITY OF LIVERPOOL

Gorton.

To traffic 12/1913.

REPAIRS:
Gor. 20/4—27/7/18.**G**.
Gor. 30/4—28/5/21.**G**.
Ross pops fitted.
Gor. 14/4—26/5/23.**G**.
Gor. 24/1—2/5/25.**G**.
Gor. 14/8/26.**L**.
Converted to oil burning.
Gor. 11/12/26—12/3/27.**G**.
Converted to coal burning.
Gor. 10—31/12/27.**L**.
Gor. 7/7—25/8/28.**G**.
Gor. 26/10—14/12/29.**G**.
Gor. 13/12/30—24/1/31.**G**.
Gor. 2—30/7/32.**G**.
Gor. 22/7—19/8/33.**G**.
Gor. 25/5—29/6/35.**G**.
Gor. 26/12/36—23/1/37.**G**.
Gor. 5/3—2/4/38.**G**.
Gor. 23/7—27/8/38.**L**.
Gor. 20/1—24/2/40.**G**.
New cylinders.
Gor. 7/10—15/11/41.**G**.
Gor. 6—30/10/43.**G**.
Gor. 22/12/45—9/2/46.**G**.
Gor. 19/4/47. *Not repaired.*

BOILERS:
1551.
665 *(new)* 27/7/18.
1549 *(ex5424)* 28/5/21.
1744 *(ex5426)* 26/5/23.
309 *(exB8 5280)* 12/3/27.
388 *(ex5424)* 24/1/31.
1935 *(exB3 6169)* 30/7/32.
1933 *(exB7 5476)* 19/8/33.
356 *(exB3 6168)* 29/6/35.
3004 *(exB7 5463)* 23/1/37.
1928 *(exB7 5470)* 2/4/38.
3030 *(new)* 24/2/40.
763 *(exB8 5280)* 15/11/41.
45 *(exB7 5477)* 30/10/43.

SHEDS:
Gorton.
Ardsley 10/3/24.
Gorton 24/5/24.
Immingham 19/7/33.
Sheffield 18/2/35.
Immingham 23/7/39.
Sheffield 13/12/42.
Immingham 20/4/45.

RENUMBERED:
428c *after 26/5/23 at shed.*
5428 2/5/25.
1493 25/8/46

CONDEMNED: 19/4/47.
Cut up at Gorton.

(below) **No.423 as new, showing the special copper capped chimney fitted in anticipation of the engine going to an exhibition in Belgium. This idea was dropped and only a model was sent. Manchester (L. Rd).**

18

No.424 was one of the three originally in black goods livery and without a name. Manchester (Central) loco yard.

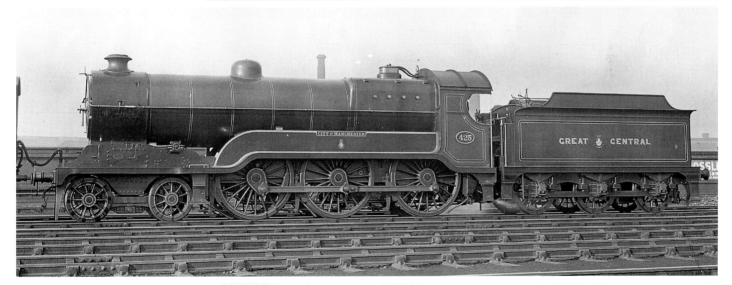

(above) All six were superheated from the start and were at first fitted with a Wakefield mechanical lubricator for the cylinders and valves. During 1917/18 all were changed to Robinson's patent 'Intensifore' sight feed lubricator.

(right) No.426 showing Ramsbottom safety valves with rectangular brass casing. Standard from the start were the whistle in front of the cab, a top lamp iron fixed on the handrail, and a wheel and handle fastening for the smokebox door.

During 1921/2 all six had their Ramsbottom safety valves replaced by Ross 'pop' type. Note that an ash ejector was also fitted at this February 1921 repair, and that steam sanding superseded the gravity type on No.427 from February 1921, the other five then being changed similarly at a later date. Guide Bridge.

No.428 showing the original arrangement for sanding by gravity. Sand could be applied in front of the leading and middle coupled wheels and also behind the rear-coupled wheels for running in reverse. For the latter there were also boxes at the front end of the tender. Manchester (London Road).

At Grouping, the arrangement for protecting the superheater elements was a combined blower and circulating valve. The latter allowed a small mount of steam to pass through the elements when the regulator was closed. To prevent unintentional movement of the engine, this steam was cleared by a header discharge valve mounted on the side of the smokebox.

By 1926, the simpler Gresley anti-vacuum valve was substituted for the Robinson arrangement and at first some had it fixed on the end of the header and so on the side of the smokebox. Gorton shed.

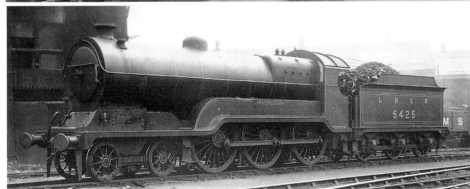

The anti-vacuum valve could be at either end of the header and as 5425 had a change of boiler in August 1927 it seems to have then acquired one with a snifter on the right hand side. Gorton shed.

The standard position for the Gresley anti-vacuum valve was at the centre of the header and thus behind the chimney. All the B2 class duly got it there, but the side position survived into the 1930's (*see* page 23, top). No move was made to bring this class within the 13ft 0in. gauge but from about 1926 they all acquired a lower dome cover. Gorton shed, October 1936.

(above) **Before Grouping a start had been made on the fitting of an ash ejector in the smokebox. For some years - at least to 1930 - the steam supply entered at the rear of the smokebox but this affected the front tube plate. Note a heater connection and hose has been fitted at the front end. Guide Bridge, 10th June 1924.**

(left) **During the 1930's the steam pipe to the ash ejector was extended to enter the front end of the smokebox and this avoided the scouring of the tube plate. Note that the top lamp iron has been moved from the rail to a more accessible position on the door, but only Nos.5424 and 5427 appear to have had this improvement. As this is clearly a photograph taken in summer the carriage warming hose had been left off. York-Harwich train at Bishopthorpe.**

The original Robinson chimney was a shapely design and served the class until the mid-1920's when it proved too susceptible to cracking.

Its replacement from about 1925 to around 1935 was the more straight sided 'plant pot' type which never seemed to suit the other Gorton design features, but all the class were so fitted. King's Cross station.

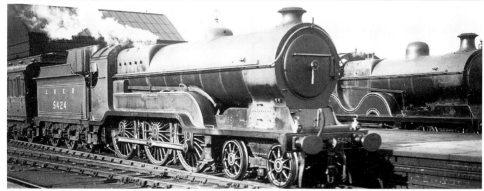

From about 1935 the whole class reverted to a much more traditional Gorton style of chimney which was retained to withdrawal. Around the same time all were fitted with hinged glass side screen on each cab side.

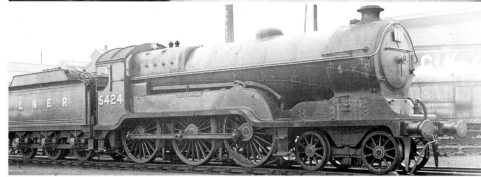

The 1926 coal strike led to four sets of Unolco oil firing apparatus being used again. They were installed on Nos.5423 from 24th July 1926 to 15th January 1927, 5424 from 31st July 1926 to 15th January 1927, 5426 from 7th August to 4th December 1926 and on 5428 from 14th August to 11th December 1926. Guide Bridge.

During 1917/18 the Wakefield mechanical lubricator for pistons and valves (*see* page 19, centre) was taken off and replaced by Robinson's Intensifore 6-feed sight-feed lubricator in the cab. Gorton shed.

23

By 1931 the Intensifore type was being replaced by Detroit or Eureka sight feed lubricator and No.5424 on 2nd July 1932 took the last B2 Intensifore to works for removal.

After 1932 there was one more modification to the cylinder lubrication. On the fireman's side of No.5427 one of the main feed pipes from the cab led into a dashpot fixed on the frame above the cylinders. By 1938 this dashpot had been discarded. Gorton shed.

The dashpot trial was extended to one more B2 but on No.5423 it was fitted on the driver's side of the engine. Scarborough shed, 1935.

Although buffer heads were still elliptical to withdrawal, those of extra width (*see* page 16, centre) were modified in early LNER years. The class retained GC design buffers, none being fitted with the Group Standard type.

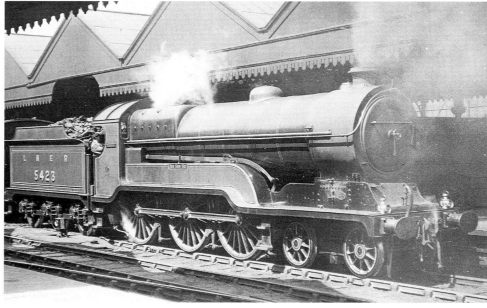

The extra two washout plugs on the shoulder of the firebox had blister type covers to them. Some kept those to withdrawal. Manchester (Central).

In its final condition No.1492 (ex 5427) after repair in December 1946, regained a lamp iron on the handrail, duplicating that on the door, had the wheel changed to another handle for the door fastening, and had the ash ejector removed. Grimsby, April 1947.

All had the usual 4000 gallon type tender and they retained their original fitting through to withdrawal. The only exception was No.5424's use of a similar J11 class tender temporarily from August 1929 to March 1930. Note that the buffers at that end had circular heads and the LNER move of the tender numberplate from the rear to the front. Note also the rear of the B7 tender on the left. Gorton shed.

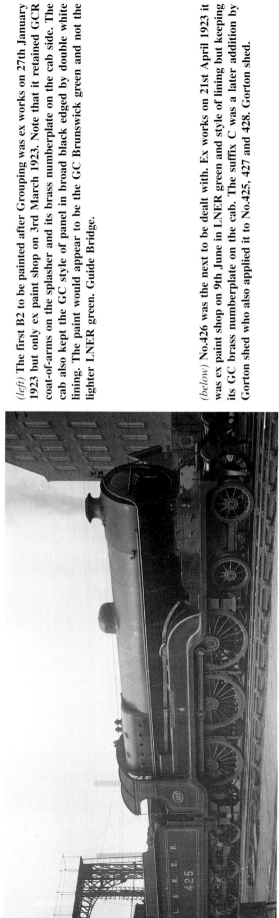

(left) The first B2 to be painted after Grouping was ex works on 27th January 1923 but only ex paint shop on 3rd March 1923. Note that it retained GCR coat-of-arms on the splasher and its brass numberplate on the cab side. The cab also kept the GC style of panel in broad black edged by double white lining. The paint would appear to be the GC Brunswick green and not the lighter LNER green. Guide Bridge.

(below) No.426 was the next to be dealt with. Ex works on 21st April 1923 it was ex paint shop on 9th June in LNER green and style of lining but keeping its GC brass numberplate on the cab. The suffix C was a later addition by Gorton shed who also applied it to No.425, 427 and 428. Gorton shed.

The third 1923 painting was No.428 in the same style as 426 but with the tender letters changed to LNER instead of L.&N.E.R. Ex works on 26th May 1923 the paint shop released it on 14th July 1923. Here, in 1923, it has called at Worksop whilst working a train from Manchester to Cleethorpes.

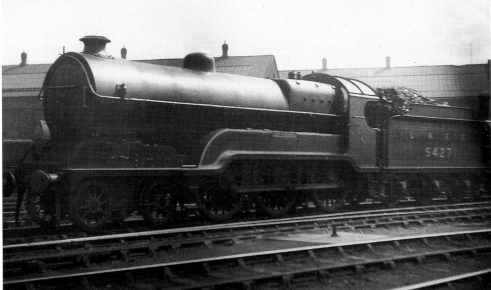

The other three went directly to LNER livery and numbering. No.5424, ex works 1st March, ex paint shop 22nd March 1924; No.5423, ex works 26th July, ex paint shop 16th August 1924; No.5427, ex works 7th March 1925, ex paint shop same day (by now Gorton was combining erecting and paint shop periods into one shopping). The first three got their LNER numbers as follows: 5425 (13th September 1924), 5426 (21st March 1925) and 5428 (2nd May 1925). Gorton shed, May 1925.

From February 1929 the number was to be put on cab instead of on the tender. B2 class were so altered at these dates in 1929:- 5423 14th September, 5424 27th April, 5425 13th April, 5427 20th April and 5428 14th December. No.5426 was altered on 24th May 1930. They continued in lined green passenger livery until during WW2 but 5427 lost its name in September 1937 when the streamlined B17 No.2870 became CITY OF LONDON. Sheffield (Neepsend) shed, 2nd July 1939.

During the war their livery became unlined black and with only NE on the tender. Nos.5424 and 5426 did not take part in the 1946 renumbering but 5425 became No.1491 on 22nd December 1946 at Immingham shed and was withdrawn as shown on 4th July 1947. No.5423 was made 1490 on 8th December 1946 also at Immingham shed and was withdrawn on 19th April 1947 still with only NE on its tender. Immingham shed, April 1947.

Only one regained LNER with original numbering, No.5428 on 9th February 1946 but the unlined black paint was still used. Note change from wheel to another handle on the smokebox door, but retention of a lamp iron on the handrail. The ash ejector had been removed but a circular plate for access to the superheater header was now provided.

The other to regain LNER was No.1492 (ex 5427 on 19th August 1946) after it was the last one to have a general repair. It was ex works on 14th December 1946 in unlined black with yellow painted and unshaded characters of Gill sans style but with a modified 9. It too had lost the ash ejector and the wheel on the smokebox door had given place to a second handle. The last of the class, it was withdrawn on 14th November 1947 after being the only unnamed one for ten years. Lincoln, July 1947.

No.5428 was renumbered 1493 by Immingham shed on 25th August 1946 and was withdrawn on 19th April 1947. Gorton works, March 1947.

No.423 was shedded at Gorton at Grouping and became No.5423 on 26th July 1924. It went to Neasden on 25th September but returned to Gorton on 12th November 1924 and from there is working a Manchester to Cleethorpes express whilst fitted for burning oil fuel during the period 24th July 1926 to 15th January 1927.

On 27th January 1930 No.5423 moved to Sheffield but went back to Gorton on 16th September only to be sent to Sheffield again on 9th December to stay there for 2½ years before going to Immingham on 27th June 1933. From there on 14th April 1934 it worked to King's Cross with a cup final special and here is backing out of the station to be prepared for the return journey.

From Immingham in 1938 No.5423 is seen at Northolt Park working this boat train special to Marylebone with passengers from a cruise liner which had called at the dock on the Humber. For part of the war it went to Sheffield on 21st November 1942 but returned to Immingham on 5th May 1945 to become No.1490 on 8th December 1946 prior to its withdrawal on 19th April 1947.

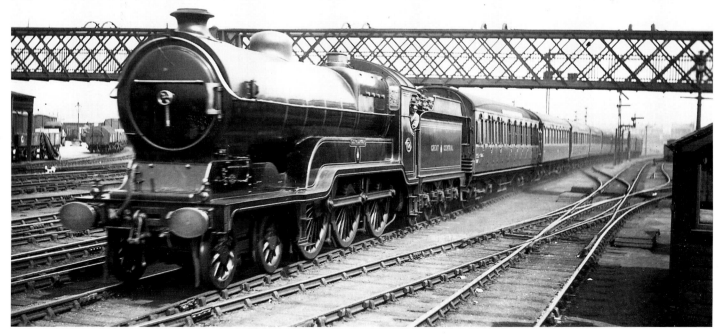

No.424 built January 1913, was at Gorton at Grouping and here at Guide Bridge is working from Sheffield to Manchester on a train from Marylebone. Note the leading coach is fitted with anti-collision buffers to prevent over-riding and telescoping.

(left) The third engine built in February 1913 became No.5425 from 16th August 1924 and worked from Gorton shed until 10th June 1933. Here on a stopping train to Sheffield it is at Manchester (Central). As 425c it was loaned to King's Cross shed on 1st June 1924 to 8th June 1924 for the first week's running of the Sheffield Pullman train.

(below) On 10th June 1933 No.5425 moved to Immingham but on 22nd February 1935 went to Sheffield and then began regular working to Hull on the 4.45 p.m. arrival and 6.30 p.m. return, both Liverpool (Central) through trains. Here in Botanic Gardens shed yard it has been turned to go back to Paragon station for the 6.30 p.m. departure.

The fourth engine built in March 1913 became No.5426 on 21st March 1925 and was at Gorton until 9th September 1930, working Manchester to Sheffield trains. It moved to Sheffield on 9th September 1930 and then Immingham from 4th May 1933 to 27th February 1935 when Sheffield had it again to 20th July 1939. In the 1930's both by Sheffield and Immingham sheds, 5426's most frequent use was on the Cleethorpes trains as here leaving Retford with the 2.20 p.m. from Cleethorpes to Manchester. Immingham got it on 20th July 1939, loaned it to Langwith Jct. on 29th May to 28th June 1942 and to Sheffield on 21st November to 13th December 1942 but still had it when withdrawn on 22nd December 1944, the first of the class to be condemned.

No.427 was also built in March 1913 and worked from Gorton with three short breaks until 22nd June 1939. No.5427 from 7th March 1925, it worked mainly from Manchester to and from Cleethorpes both via Retford and via Doncaster. It went to Immingham on 25th April 1928 but returned to Gorton on 15th December. Gorton sent 5427 to Sheffield for two spells on 24th November 1929 to 24th November 1930 and 2nd May to 26th June 1933 but from either it worked mainly Manchester to Sheffield passenger trains. Here, in March 1933, it is over the ash pit at Gorton shed after refuelling.

Here at Manchester (Central) 5427 is about to go to Sheffield with the portion from Liverpool of the boat train to Harwich. On 22nd June 1939, No.5427 went to Lincoln and then to Immingham on 21st November 1942 and was numbered to 1492 on 19th August 1946.

In the period June to October 1920, five more were built, Nos.1164 and 1166 with the same type of cab as No.1169, but Nos.1165, 1167 and 1168 had double window cabs with a rearward extension to the roof. At Grouping at least Nos.1165, 1167 and 1168 still had both methods of protecting the superheater elements, however, by 1925 No.6165 had lost the header discharge valve but had retained the external control to blower valve. Nottingham (Victoria).

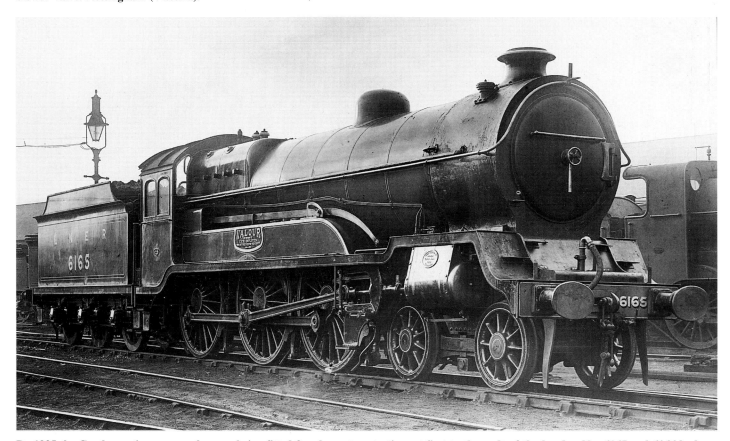

By 1925 the Gresley anti-vacuum valve was being fitted for element protection, at first to the ends of the header. Nos.6165 and 6166 had one at both ends although one sufficed on the others, normally on the right hand side. King's Cross shed, 1925.

CLASS B 3

6169

LORD FARINGDON

Gorton.

To traffic 11/1917.

REPAIRS:
Gor. 7/3—29/4/22.**G.**
Gor. 7—14/4/23.**H.**
Valves & pistons
Gor. 28/7—25/8/23.**G.**
Gor. 2/5—27/6/25.**G.**
Gor. 27/3—17/4/26.**L.**
Gor. 28/5—23/7/27.**G.**
Gor. 10/11/28—2/2/29.**G.**
Gor. 29/3—10/5/30.**G.**
Gor. 26/3—30/4/32.**G.**
Gor. 1—8/10/32.**L.**
Gor. 29/4—17/6/33.**G.**
Gor. 4/8—1/9/34.**G.**
Gor. 16/5—13/6/36.**G.**
Gor. 5/2—5/3/38.**G.**
Gor. 28/10—18/11/39.**G.**
Gor. 4/9—10/10/42.**G.**
Gor. 27/11—26/12/42.**L.**
New R.H. outside cylinder.
Gor. 10/10—4/11/44.**G.**
Gor. 29/9/45.**L.**
Gor. 1/6—27/7/46.**G.**
Gor. 6/12/47. *Not repaired.*

BOILERS:
1712.
  599 (*exB8 5445*) 29/4/22.
1846 (*ex6165*) 27/6/25.
1935 (*ex6166*) 10/5/30.
  556 (*exB7 5458*) 30/4/32.
  579 (*exB2 5424*) 13/6/36.
3001 (*exB7 5466*) 5/3/38.
  242 (*ex6166*) 18/11/39.
3015 (*exB7 5468*) 10/10/42.
3047 (*new*) 27/7/46.

SHEDS:
Gorton.
Immingham.
King's Cross 8/23.
Mexborough 11/23.
Copley Hill 15/5/24.
King's Cross 11/8/25.
Gorton 27/9/25.
Copley Hill 10/10/25.
King's Cross 12/12/25.
Copley Hill 2/27.
Gorton 21/4/27.
Neasden 24/10/27.

Gorton 7/11/28.
Neasden 2/3/29.
Immingham 15/5/30.
Neasden 20/3/33.
Immingham 17/6/33.
Gorton 18/9/33.
Immingham 11/12/35.
Woodford 21/7/39.
Copley Hill 12/7/42.
Gorton 24/12/42.
Neasden 24/12/44.
Immingham 16/4/45.
Lincoln 1/6/47.

RENUMBERED:
1169c 25/8/23.
6169 27/6/25.
1494 1/9/46.

CONDEMNED: 6/12/47.
Cut up at Dukinfield.

6164

EARL BEATTY

Gorton.

To traffic 6/1920.

REPAIRS:
Gor. 13/5—24/6/22.**G.**
Gor. 29/9—15/12/23.**G.**
Gor. 25/4—11/7/25.**G.**
Gor. 30/10/26—19/2/27.**G.**
New inside cylinders.
Intensifore changed to 6-feed
Eureka split to 10 points.
Gor. 11/8—10/11/28.**G.**
New inside cylinders.
Gor. 14/9—19/10/29.**G.**
Gor. 4/10—15/11/30.**G.**
Gor. 12—31/12/31.**G.**
Gor. 12—26/11/32.**G.**
Gor. 13/1—10/2/34.**G.**
Gor. 30/3—13/4/35.**G.**
Gor. 24/10—14/11/36.**G.**
Gor. 5/3—2/4/38.**G.**
Gor. 8/4—24/6/39.**G.**
Rebuilt to Part 2.
Gor. 26/10—23/11/40.**G.**
Gor. 19/8—20/9/41.**L.**
Gor. 24/12/42—13/2/43.**G.**
Gor. 2/12/44—13/1/45.**G.**

BOILERS:
1845.
1712 (*ex6169*) 24/6/22.

406 (*exB8 5444*) 15/12/23.
610 (*exB7 5038*) 19/10/29.
1846 (*ex6169*) 15/11/30.
  267 (*exB7 5468*) 31/12/31.
1927 (*exB7 5477*) 26/11/32.
  51 (*new*) 10/2/34.
  59 (*exB7 5465*) 13/4/35.
  244 (*exB7 5484*) 14/11/36.
3004 (*exB2 5428*) 2/4/38.
3017 (*exB7 5467*) 24/6/39.
  534 (*exB7 5474*) 23/11/40.
3045 (*new*) 13/1/45.

SHEDS:
Gorton.
Immingham 22/10/20.
King's Cross 15/2/24.
Copley Hill 5/8/24.
King's Cross 23/7/25.
Copley Hill 5/10/25.
King's Cross 8/11/25.
Gorton 23/2/27.
Immingham 12/12/28.
Neasden 6/12/30.
Gorton 5/12/34.
Immingham 13/4/35.
Woodford 24/7/39.
Copley Hill 3/4/42.
Woodford 19/7/42.
Gorton 21/11/42.
Neasden 13/2/43.
Immingham 28/6/47.

RENUMBERED:
1164c 15/12/23.
6164 11/7/25.
1495 7/10/46.

CONDEMNED: 27/9/47.
Cut up at Gorton.

6165

VALOUR

Gorton.

To traffic 7/1920.

REPAIRS:
Gor. 25/2—1/4/22.**G.**
Gor. 23/6—11/8/23.**G.**
Ex works in full GC livery
(only touched up).
Gor. 15/11/24—31/1/25.**G.**
Gor. 11—18/4/25.**L.**
Gor. 31/10—14/11/25.**L.**
Gor. 2/4—4/6/27.**G.**

Gor. 14/7—15/9/28.**G.**
Gor. 13/10/28.**L.**
Gor. 12/4—7/6/30.**G.**
Gor. 24/10—7/11/31.**G.**
Gor. 30/4—14/5/33.**L.**
Side screens fitted.
Gor. 29/4—27/5/33.**G.**
Gor. 21/7—18/8/34.**G.**
Gor. 14/9—12/10/35.**G.**
Gor. 10/4—8/5/37.**G.**
Gor. 27/8—15/10/38.**G.**
Gor. 18/5—15/6/40.**G.**
Gor. 4—30/5/42.**G.**
Gor. 29/4—27/5/44.**G.**
Gor. 4/5—15/6/46.**G.**
Gor. 31/12/47. *Not repaired.*

BOILERS:
1846.
1712 (*ex6164*) 31/1/25.
1849 (*exB2 5423*) 4/6/27.
  571 (*new*) 7/11/31.
  295 (*exB7 5033*) 27/5/33.
  773 (*new*) 18/8/34.
3005 (*exB7 5036*) 8/5/37.
  631 (*exB7 5461*) 15/10/38.
3003 (*exB8 5444*) 15/6/40.
3038 (*new*) 30/5/42.
3033 (*exB8 5004*) 15/6/46.

SHEDS:
Gorton.
King's Cross 11/8/23.
Copley Hill 6/10/25.
King's Cross 27/11/25.
Gorton 28/3/27.
Immingham 15/12/28.
Neasden 14/11/31.
Immingham 3/6/32.
Neasden 21/4/33.
Gorton 6/12/34.
Immingham 21/2/35.
Neasden 7/12/35.
Immingham 28/11/38.
Woodford 25/7/39.
Copley Hill 25/3/42.
Gorton 21/11/42.
Neasden 24/12/44.
Immingham 16/4/45.
Lincoln 1/6/47.

RENUMBERED:
6165 31/1/25.
1496 1/9/46.

CONDEMNED: 31/12/47.
Cut up at Dukinfield.

WORKS CODES:- Cw - Cowlairs. Dar- Darlington. Don - Doncaster. Ghd - Gateshead. Gor - Gorton. Inv - Inverurie. Str - Stratford.
REPAIR CODES:- **C/H** - Casual Heavy. **C/L** - Casual Light. **G** - General. **H**- Heavy. **H/I** - Heavy Intermediate. **L** - Light. **L/I** - Light Intermediate. **N/C** - Non-Classified.

The standard central position behind the chimney had been adopted by 1929 and thereafter all six were so fitted.

For about two months in the summer of 1921, Nos.1165, 1167 and 1169 were fitted to burn oil on the Unolco system but no B3 was so fitted during the 1926 coal strike. Note Reliostop train control fitment on the tender between the first and second axles. This was removed during 1922. Guide Bridge.

All six originally had 12-feed Intensifiore for main lubrication, and retained it until after the LNER took over. The last to have it was 6165 to October 1931.

In February 1927 on Nos.6164 and 6166 a change to Eureka or Detroit lubrication began. This was 6-feed with three pipes from the cab on each side of the boiler. Northolt Junction, 1933.

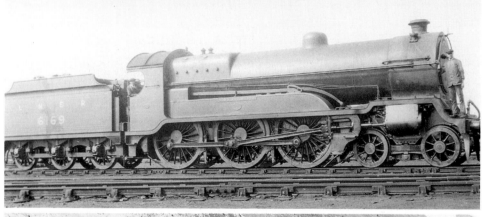

The three feeds on the right hand side were arranged in exactly the same manner.

By 1935, Nos.6164, 6165 and 6167 had part of the lubrication on the left hand side changed to a Wakefield mechanical type and 6169 was so equipped later. Apart from 6167 the Wakefield was then retained. Note that cab side screens were now fitted. Nottingham (Victoria).

Only on the left hand side was there a change to Wakefield mechanical lubricator.

During the 1939-45 war the lubricator pipes were taken off the right hand side of 6169. Note a second handle has replaced the wheel for fastening the smokebox door and a gangway door has been added between engine and tender. Nos.6169 (1494) and 6165 (1496) retained the lamp iron fixed on the handrail over the door of the smokebox. Spalding, April 1947.

The original chimneys were all of Robinson's shapely design, but these, as on other classes, proved to be susceptible to cracking. Neasden shed.

6166

EARL HAIG

Gorton.

To traffic 8/1920.

REPAIRS:
Gor. 28/1—25/3/22.**G.**
Gor. 26/5—16/6/23.**L.**
Valves & pistons.
Gor. 23/2—7/6/24.**G.**
Gor. 8/8—7/11/25.**G.**
Gor. 20/11/26—12/2/27.**G.**
Gor. 3—24/9/27.**L.**
Gor. 23/6—6/10/28.**G.**
Gor. 19/10—31/12/29.**G.**
Rebuilt to Part 2.
Gor. 5—19/4/30.**L.**
Gor. 15—22/11/30.**L.**
Gor. 17/1—7/2/31.**G.**
Gor. 15/8—5/9/31.**L.**
Gor. 30/1—27/2/32.**G.**
Gor. 18/2—11/3/33.**G.**
Gor. 24/2—7/4/34.**G.**
Gor. 8/12/34.**L.**
Lubricator position changed.
Gor. 13/7—10/8/35.**G.**
Gor. 28/11—26/12/36.**G.**
Gor. 27/2/37.**L.**
Gor. 7/5—2/7/38.**G.**
Gor. 14/10—4/11/39.**G.**
Gor. 19/10/40.**L.**
Gor. 11—28/6/41.**L.**
Gor. 2/2—9/10/43.**G.**
Rebuilt to Part 3.
Nameplate removed.
Gor. 24/2—4/3/44.**L.**
Frame cracked.
Gor. 27/5—3/6/44.**L.**
Gor. 6—27/1/45.**L.**
Gor. 7/7—25/8/45.**H.**
Gor. 30/11/46—25/1/47.**H.**
Gor. 18/10/47.**L.**
Gor. 3—24/4/48.**L.**
Gor. 4—18/9/48.**L.**

BOILERS:
1847.
  534 *(new)* 7/6/24.
1935 *(ex6168)* 6/10/28.
  397 *(exB7 5472)* 31/12/29.
    8 *(new)* 7/2/31.
1846 *(ex6164)* 27/2/32.
  274 *(exB7 5483)* 11/3/33.
  571 *(exB7 5472)* 7/4/34.
1933 *(exB2 5428)* 10/8/35.
  242 *(exB8 5445)* 26/12/36.
1932 *(exB7 5469)* 4/11/39.
9428 *(new)* 9/10/43.

SHEDS:
Gorton.
Doncaster 20/7/23.

King's Cross 26/7/23.
Gorton 13/2/24.
Copley Hill 30/6/24.
King's Cross 12/11/24.
Copley Hill 4/10/25.
King's Cross 27/11/25.
Gorton 12/2/27.
Neasden 23/10/27.
Gorton 9/10/28.
Neasden 5/11/28.
Gorton 11/3/33.
Neasden 12/12/35.
Gorton 8/10/43.
Neasden 1/11/45.
Immingham 14/7/47.

RENUMBERED:
6166 7/6/24.
1497 28/9/46.
61497 24/4/48.

CONDEMNED: 14/4/49.
Cut up at Dukinfield.

6167

LLOYD GEORGE

Gorton.

To traffic 9/1920.

REPAIRS:
Gor. 29/7—26/8/22.**G.**
Gor. 20—30/8/23.**N/C.**
After removal of nameplates at
King's Cross shed.
Gor. 26/4—5/7/24.**G.**
Gor. 5/9—21/11/25.**G.**
Gor. 28/5—30/7/27.**G.**
Gor. 18/8—1/12/28.**G.**
Gor. 8/2—8/3/30.**G.**
Gor. 30/5—27/6/31.**G.**
Gor. 18/2—4/3/33.**G.**
Gor. 31/3—21/4/34.**G.**
Gor. 7—28/3/36.**G.**
Gor. 9/4—25/6/38.**G.**
Rebuilt to Part 2.
Gor. 27/5—17/6/39.**L.**
Gor. 20/4—1/6/40.**G.**
Gor. 10/6—31/7/43.**G.**
Gor. 27/7—21/9/46.**G.**
Gor. 31/12/47. *Not repaired.*

BOILERS:
1848.
1849 *(ex6168)* 26/8/22.
1847 *(ex6166)* 5/7/24.
1924 *(exB7 5458)* 21/11/25.
  69 *(exB7 5073)* 30/7/27.
1930 *(exB7 5464)* 1/12/28.
1932 *(exB7 5032)* 27/6/31.
1924 *(exB7 5458)* 4/3/33.
  81 *(new)* 21/4/34.
  300 *(exB7 5480)* 28/3/36.

  579 *(ex6169)* 25/6/38.
3015 *(ex6169)* 21/9/46.

SHEDS:
Gorton.
King's Cross 2/8/23.
Immingham 12/23.
King's Cross 5/8/24.
Copley Hill 5/8/25.
King's Cross 12/12/25.
Gorton 7/3/27.
Neasden 14/6/29.
Immingham 16/7/31.
Neasden 16/12/32.
Gorton 1/2/35.
Immingham 1/3/35.
Neasden 29/11/38.
Immingham 26/6/47.

RENUMBERED:
1167c ?/9/23.
6167 5/7/24.
1498 21/9/46.

CONDEMNED: 31/12/47.
Cut up at Dukinfield.

6168

LORD STUART OF
WORTLEY

Gorton.

To traffic 10/1920.

REPAIRS:
Gor. 1—29/7/22.**G.**
Gor. 8/12/23—1/3/24.**G.**
Gor. 25/7—31/10/25.**G.**
Gor. 19/2—16/4/27.**G.**
Gor. 28/4—30/6/28.**G.**
Gor. 22/6—21/9/29.**G.**
Rebuilt to Part 2.
Gor. 14/12/29.**L.**
Gor. 18/1/30.**L.**
Gor. 10—17/5/30.**L.**
Gor. 25/10—1/11/30.**L.**
Steam chest gauge fitted.
Gor. 7/2—28/3/31.**G.**
Gor. 1—8/8/31.**L.**
Gor. 7—21/11/31.**L.**
Gor. 3/9—8/10/32.**G.**
Gor. 14—21/10/33.**L.**
Gor. 28/4—9/6/34.**G.**
Gor. 15/12/34.**L.**
Lubricator position changed.
Gor. 4/5—1/6/35.**G.**
Gor. 25/7—29/8/36.**G.**
New right & left cylinders.
Gor. 13—27/3/37.**H.**
Gor. 18/6—6/8/38.**G.**
Gor. 24/2—30/3/40.**G.**
Gor. 30/11—21/12/40.**L.**
Gor. 4/9—10/10/42.**G.**

Gor. 27/5—24/6/44.**G.**
Gor. 28/9/46. *Not repaired.*

BOILERS:
1849.
1845 *(ex6164)* 29/7/22.
1935 *(exB7 5035)* 31/10/25.
1929 *(exB7 5463)* 30/6/28.
  80 *(exB7 5466)* 21/9/29.
  355 *(exB7 5483)* 28/3/31.
  356 *(exB7 5466)* 8/10/32.
  65 *(exB7 5461)* 1/6/35.
3014 *(new)* 29/8/36.
3022 *(new)* 6/8/38.
3010 *(exB7 5460)* 30/3/40.
3002 *(exB8 5279)* 10/10/42.
3035 *(exB7 5483)* 24/6/44.

SHEDS:
Gorton.
Immingham *by* 4/22.
King's Cross 16/4/24.
Copley Hill 27/4/25.
Gorton 16/4/27.
Immingham 14/5/27.
Neasden 20/7/28.
Gorton 14/6/29.
Neasden 5/2/30.
Gorton 21/2/30.
Neasden 3/3/30.
Gorton 21/3/33.
Neasden 12/3/36.

RENUMBERED:
6168 1/3/24.
1499 *allocated.*

CONDEMNED: 28/9/46.
Cut up at Gorton.

Beginning with No.6169 in June 1925, all were changed to the built up 'plant pot' type.

(*above*) Around 1935 there was a reversion to a cast type closely resembling the original shape and all six were so changed. Nottingham (Victoria).

(*right*) Domes fitted on the original boilers were only 1¼in. below chimney height and were 13ft 2⁷⁄₁₆in. above rail level. King's Cross shed, June 1925.

41

On this class no effort was made to bring it within the 13ft 0in. load gauge. The shorter dome was the result of boiler exchanging with the B7 class. Nottingham (Victoria).

(opposite, top) In September 1929, No.6168 was rebuilt with Caprotti poppet valve gear and initiated Part 2 of the Class. Note alteration to the handrail on the smokebox, with the top lamp iron now fixed on the door. Trials showed a 16% lower coal consumption. The smokebox door cross rail was moved higher to match ends of rail on sides. No.6166 became Part 2 in January 1930 (ex works 31st December 1929) and also had its cam boxes fully cased to keep out grit and dirt. Neasden shed.

The last use of one of the original boilers was on 6166 to February 1933, and that had already been changed to a low dome. All replacement boilers - this one was built in 1941 - had a low dome to facilitate use by B2, B3, B7 and B8 class engines. Sheffield (Victoria), 6th August 1945.

A smokebox ash ejector was an original fitting, the steam pipe for it entering at the rear of the box. In 1924/5 the whole class exchanged tenders with D11 class Nos.5501 to 5505 and 5511. These 1922 built tenders were self-trimming and of the same capacity, so needed sides further apart giving less flare to the coping. These later tenders also had standard axle boxes whereas the original B3 tenders had Iracier type with shield shape covers *(see page 37)*.

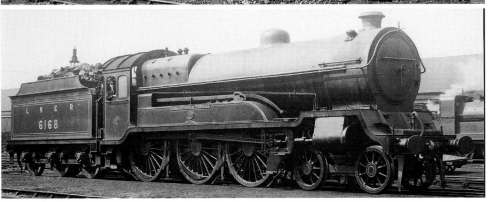

Steam for the ash ejector at the rear of the smokebox led to scouring of the front tube-plate so from 1925 the pipe was extended to enter at the front of the smokebox and all were so altered. No.6166 lost the ash ejector in 1943 when rebuilt to Part 3 and it was removed from No.6169 (1494) when last repaired in July 1946, also from 6165 (1496) in June 1946, and 1498 in September 1946. The other two still had it at withdrawal. King's Cross shed.

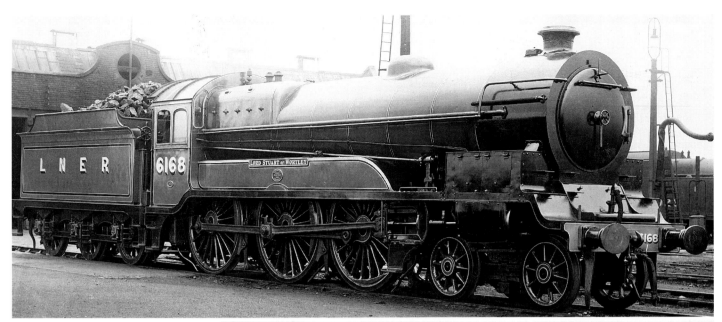

(right) Full enclosure of the cam boxes caused overheating and by 1934 ventilating holes were drilled in the front end and the side panels were taken off. Note the cross rail has been restored to lower position and lamp iron moved off the door. Neasden shed.

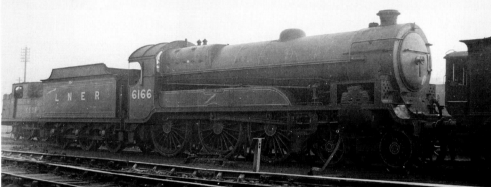

(right, lower) By July 1936 the whole of the cam box enclosures had been removed from both engines. Note smokebox door cross rail still in lower position, but the lamp iron is back on the door. Neasden shed, July 1936.

(below) By the middle 1930's, Nos.6168 and 6166 appear to have exchanged smokeboxes. 6168 now has the cross rail in the lower position as compared with the photo at the top of the page. Gorton shed, April 1936.

No.6166 reverted to its 1930 arrangement as shown on No.6168 in the illustration on the previous page, top. Both the cross rail and lamp iron differing in position from that shown in the view below on the same page. Neepsend shed.

In June 1938 No.6167 was rebuilt to Part 2 but differed from the previous two in how the Poppet valves were returned to their seats after opening. On Nos.6168 and 6166 springs were used but on 6167 steam pressure closed them. The steam was taken from the left-hand side of the dome and piped under the cladding of the boiler. One more was converted to Part 2, No.6164 in June 1939 using the same method of valve operation as on No.6167 and with smokebox rails altered similarly.

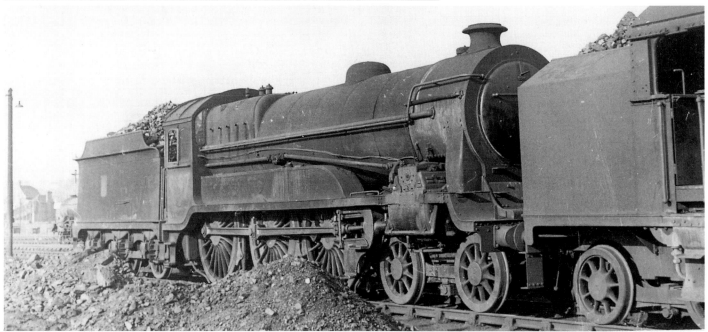

No.6167 retained the smokebox ash ejector until it went to works on 27th July 1946 but it was then taken off. Prior to that the cross rail had been put in the lower position and the lamp iron was also fitted lower down on the door. The wheel for the door fastening survived. Neasden shed, June 1946.

Externally No.6167, and No.6164 later, differed from Nos.6168 and 6166 in the shape of the covers to their outside steam pipes, but more obviously in the arrangement of their reversing rod. On 6168 and 6166 (*see* page 43, top) it was in one piece, but for 6167 and 6164 it was in two lengths connected by a universal joint, to keep it clear of the splasher. The smokebox ash ejector was not altered. The tender is not a self-trimming type, so has the more pronounced flare, but the other three Part 2 engines had the self-trimming type throughout. No.6167 had been changed to the earlier type of D11 tender in July 1927 and kept it to withdrawal. Gorton shed.

Apart from August 1925 to April 1933, No.6169 had its original tender. During the first spell, the tender had Iracier axleboxes (*see* Page 37) but these had been changed to standard when the tender was repaired in March 1928. King's Cross loco yard.

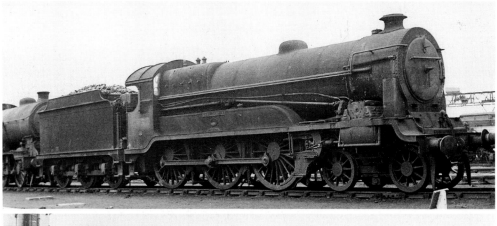

During the 1939-45 war, No.6164 (1495) had its smokebox cross rail moved to the lower position and the lamp iron was also lowered. A second handle replaced the wheel for fastening the door.

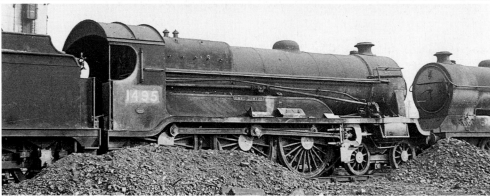

Despite these late smokebox changes, No.1495 retained its smokebox ash ejector to its withdrawal on 27th September 1947 as shown by this 12th April 1947 photograph. Its final shopping had been in January 1945. Neasden shed.

Whilst 1498 got the rail and lamp iron changes, it had the ash ejector removed when shopped in September 1946 but managed to retain the wheel and handle fastening for the smokebox door to withdrawal on 31st December 1947. Dukinfield works, March 1948.

All were in full GCR green livery at LNER take-over and there was only one small variation. Except for No.1165, the works plate was carried on the splasher below the name. On 1165 the depth of the war memorial plate did not permit this, so it was mounted on the cylinder casing. Although it had a general repair from 23rd June to 11th August 1923, the paint shop only touched up its GC livery and the change of tender to self-trimming type was to 501's tender which had Great Central on it. This GC livery was worn to 15th November 1924 when it went to works. No.1166 got 502's tender which also had Great Central and that pairing went to works on 23rd February 1924. Nottingham (Victoria).

Standard LNER livery was put on 1169c, ex paint shop on 1st September 1923, and on 1164c, ex paint shop on 12th January 1924. Although both kept the large brass GC numberplate on the cab, this plate and the regional suffix C were removed after 1164c went to works on 25th April 1925 and 1169c on 2nd May 1925 from which repairs they came out as 6164 (11th July 1925) and 6169 (27th June 1925).

In September 1923 No.1167 exchanged tenders with No.503 and the latter's tender was ex paint shop on 27th January 1923 in GC green livery but lettered L.& N.E.R. in the 4½in. size Gorton were then using. As engine 1167 was still in GC green it was only needed to change 503 to 1167 on the tender and add the area suffix C. This remained until works entry on 26th April 1924 and when ex works on 5th July 1924 it was as LNER 6167, and with only the small LNER type numberplate on the cab. Gorton shed, December 1923.

No.1166 went into Gorton on 23rd February 1924 and was there until 14th June. It was ex paint shop in standard livery except for the large brass GC style numberplate showing 6166 on the cab. No.1168 went to works on 8th December 1923 in GC livery and with its own tender. When out of the paint shop on 22nd March 1924 it was as LNER 6168 and with that number on a large brass plate on the cab. The tender was the self-trimming type from No.505 appropriately re-painted (*see* page 38, top). The large brass numberplates did not survive the next shopping, No.6166 (8th August to 7th November 1925) and No.6168 (25th July to 31st October 1925). From July 1924 to the first re-painting after February 1929, the number was carried on the tender. The last one to do so was 6165, to April 1930. King's Cross shed.

Green livery with broad black and narrow white lining continued to be used until after July 1941 and war time economies prevailed.

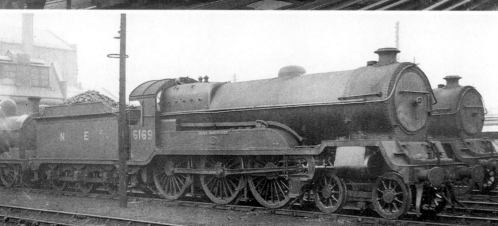

(middle) By July 1943 all six were in unlined black and with only NE on the tender. Nos. 6168 and 6164 (1495) remained this way until withdrawal. Darnall shed, May 1946.

(below) From general repairs, 6169 (27th July 1946) and 6165 (15th June 1946) came out still in unlined black but with LNER restored. On Sunday 1st September 1946, at Immingham shed, they were renumbered 1494 and 1496 by stencilling (see page 42, 2nd from top). One more regained LNER but when 6167 was ex works on 21st September 1946 it had been renumbered 1498 using normal shaded transfers (see page 46, 2nd from bottom). Dukinfield works, March 1948.

On 2nd February 1943 No.6166 went into Gorton needing new cylinders; it came out on 9th October 1943 a very different engine and re-classed as Part 3. Thompson's standardisation plans included rebuilding all B7 and B17 engines to two cylinders and using the diagram 100A boiler. 6166 was the guinea pig for this and from the engine which went in only the bogie, driving wheels, rear part of frame and the tender survived. A complete B1 class front end, cylinders, motion, boiler and cab, also chimney and Group Standard buffers were grafted on and the bogie was set 11in. nearer to the coupled wheels. Only the angular dome cover, and swivelling draw hook were reminders of its Gorton origin. It remained an only one. Gorton shed.

No.6166 was almost a B1 class engine except for its 6ft 9in. coupled wheels. It had been reallocated to Gorton shed on 8th October 1943 but due to early trouble with cracked frames they used it mainly on local passenger work. After an August 1945 heavy repair, 6166 moved to Neasden on 1st November 1945 and here on 10th September 1946 is at Moor Park near Rickmansworth. Even from that shed it was not recorded on any express work. On Saturday 28th September 1946 Neasden changed its number to 1497.

Despite considerable trouble from cracked frames this oddment (6166) was given respectable treatment. From a heavy repair it was ex Gorton on 25th January 1947 in fully lined LNER green livery but with yellow painted numbers and letters, without shading in Gill sans except for the modified 9. Note that the tender did not change to Group Standard buffers and it remained the self trimming type which had been with this engine from September 1923. Gorton works, March 1948.

In Gorton from the 3rd to 24th April 1948, for a light repair, it got BRITISH RAILWAYS in place of LNER and also acquired its BR number on the cab and buffer beam including modified 6 and 9. Note 12in. numbers but 10in. lettering. Immingham shed, May 1948.

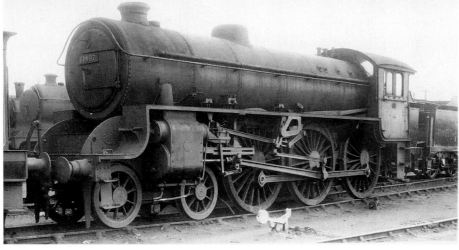

On 18th September 1948, from another light repair, it was ex Gorton fitted with a numberplate on the smokebox which also included modified 6 and 9. It was withdrawn as such on 14th April 1949 and sent for cutting up at Dukinfield. Gorton works.

No.1169 built November 1917 began at Gorton but in 1921 went to Immingham and after Grouping from May to July 1923, was tried on GN mainline work by King's Cross shed. In works on 28th July to 25th August it was out as LNER 1169c and again worked from King's Cross until November 1923 and after a spell at Mexborough, on 15th May 1924 was allocated to Copley Hill. Whilst on the G.N. line, its work was mainly on the Harrogate Pullman between King's Cross and Leeds (Central), as here at Belle Isle after it changed to 6169 from 27th June 1925. From 11th August 1925 to 27th September it was at King's Cross shed then went to Gorton shed but only to 10th October when Copley Hill got it again until 12th December. It was again at King's Cross shed from 12th December 1925 still on the Pullman working to and from Leeds. It was sent back to Copley Hill in February 1927 and by then Classes C1 and D11 had been found suitable and more economical on the Pullman. So on 21st April 1927 it returned to work on the GC from Gorton shed. It only had one more spell at an ex GN shed - from the 12th July to 24th December 1942 at Copley Hill.

Back on the GC it did not find ready acceptance, no shed keeping it longer than three years and in its remaining 20½ years it was transferred no less than fourteen times between Gorton, Neasden and Immingham with Woodford, Copley Hill and Lincoln each having it once. Here in 1931 at Bagthorpe Junction it has a Marylebone to Immingham boat train. It was at Gorton from 21st April to 24th October 1927, 7th November 1928 to 2nd March 1929 and 18th September 1933 to 11th December 1935; Neasden from 24th October 1927 to 7th November 1928, 2nd March 1929 to 15th May 1930 and 20th March to 17th June 1933; Immingham from 15th May 1930 to 20th March 1933, 17th June to 18th September 1933 and 11th December 1935 to 21st July 1939. At Woodford from 21st July 1939 it stayed until 12th July 1942 when Copley Hill then had it until 24th December. After exactly two years at Gorton on 24th December 1944 it moved to Neasden then on 16th April 1945 to Immingham, who on Sunday 1st September 1946 changed its number to 1494. Finally it was at Lincoln from 1st June to its 6th December 1947 withdrawal.

No.1164, built in June 1920, began work at Gorton, then went to Immingham on 22nd October 1920. In December 1923 it moved to King's Cross to be used on the Pullman working from 15th February 1924 until 23rd February 1927 when it was returned to the GC Section. For the Pullmans it had two spells from the Leeds end, being shedded at Copley Hill on 5th August 1924 to 23rd July 1925 and 5th October to 8th November 1925, returning to King's Cross each time. From 11th July 1925 it was 6164 and King's Cross used it other than just on the Harrogate Pullman as here with an up excursion with the train made up of a pair of quad–art suburban sets used in the London area. Back on the G.C. at Gorton from 23rd February 1927, No.6164 found it difficult to settle but it did have two spells each of 4 years at Neasden from 6th December 1930 to 5th December 1934 and 13th February 1943 to 28th June 1947. For GC main line work it was also at Gorton on 23rd February 1927 to 12th December 1928, 5th December 1934 to 13th April 1935 and 21st November 1942 to 13th February 1943.

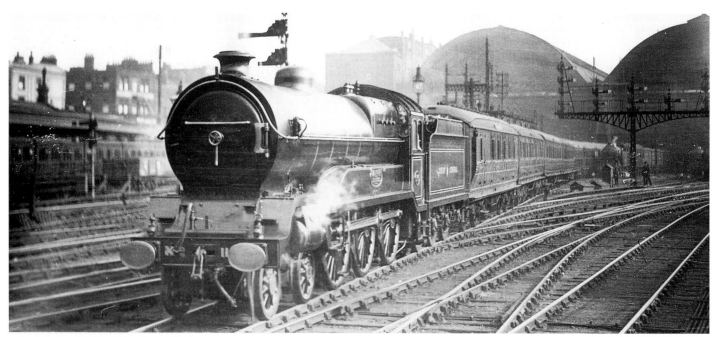

No.1165, built in July 1920, worked from Gorton until 11th August 1923 when it moved to King's Cross shed. In April 1923 the LNER appointed a GCR man W.G.P. Maclure as Locomotive Running Superintendent of the Southern Area and at his instigation B3 class were drafted to the GN line to work important trains to and from Leeds as Pacifics were not then allowed on the Doncaster to Leeds section. From 31st January 1925 it was 6165 and it often hauled the Harrogate Pullman to and from Leeds. From 6th October to 27th November 1925 it was at Leeds Copley Hill shed but returned to King's Cross until on 28th March 1927 it went back to the GC at Gorton shed. Whilst at Gorton in 1927/1928, No.6165 could still be seen in London on Manchester expresses. Indeed it had four spells working from Neasden shed from 14th November 1931 to 3rd June 1932, 21st April 1933 to 6th December 1934, also 7th December 1935 to 28th November 1938 and 24th December 1944 to 16th April 1945. Like its fellows, it moved frequently having fifteen transfers in the 1927-1947 period.

After its return to GC workings from Gorton, No.6165 also worked Manchester to Cleethorpes trains as here climbing to Woodhead and on 15th December 1928 it moved to Immingham for the first of six allocations there up to June 1947. From 25th July 1939 No.6165 moved to Woodford until 25th March 1942 when it was at Copley Hill again but only to 21st November when it went to Gorton. On Sunday 1st September 1946 Immingham changed it to 1496 (*see* photo 37 page XX) and on 1st June 1947 sent it to Lincoln from where it was withdrawn on 31st December.

After being rebuilt with Poppet valves, 6168 spent some months at Gorton shed so that adjustments could be easily made whilst the equipment settled down. On 3rd March 1930 it moved to Neasden for three years of main line expresses duties after which it moved on the 21st March 1933 to Gorton shed to do similar work from that end for another three years before, on 12th March 1936, it returned to Neasden and - most unusually for B3 class - remained at that shed until it was withdrawn on 28th September 1946. From its 1936 return to Neasden it does not seem to have had the onerous duties, these being taken by B17/4 and the A1 classes. It did however work quite often to Leicester on the 10.00 a.m. Marylebone to Bradford, returning in the afternoon with the 1.50 p.m. all-stations train as seen here at Harrow in 1938. The Poppet valve engines were said to be reliable and to average 50,000 miles each year. In the Thompson renumbering 6168 was to have been 1499 but it was not applied before 6168 was withdrawn.

Only one of the class was named. In July 1906 No.1097 worked the special train carrying notabilities to the cutting of the first sod for the new dock at Immingham. It was given that name and carried it to withdrawal. Note rectangular brass casing to safety valves.

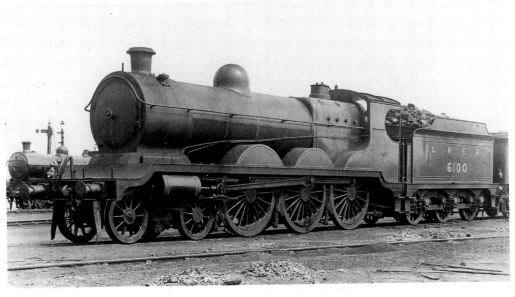

(above) Between April 1925 (6101) and October 1928 (6098) all ten were superheated and were fitted with Gresley anti-vacuum valves. At the same time as they changed to superheater, three, Nos.6104 (March), 6103 (May) and 6095 (October), all in 1927, were fitted with 21in. cylinders and piston valves. Nottingham (Victoria) south turntable.

(left) On the first three to be superheated, Nos. 6101 (April 1925), 6100 (January 1926) and 6097 (May 1926), the Gresley anti-vacuum valve was fitted at the end of the header, but they were soon changed to the central position as on the others. Annesley, June 1926.

CLASS B 4

6095

Beyer, Peacock 4816.

To traffic 6/1906.

REPAIRS:
Gor. 30/3—11/5/07.**G.**
Gor. 22/11/10—4/2/11.**G.**
Gor. 18/10—22/11/13.**G.**
Gor. 4/9—9/10/20.**G.**
Gor. 8/7—30/9/22.**G.**
Gor. 29/11/24—21/2/25.**G.**
Gor. 9/7—8/10/27.**G.**
Superheated boiler & new 21in.
P.V. cylinders fitted.
Gor. 5/4—17/5/30.**G.**
Gor. 23/4—28/5/32.**G.**
Gor. 20/5—3/6/33.**G.**
Gor. 28/7—4/8/34.**L.**
Gor. 12—26/1/35.**G.**
Gor. 4—25/4/36.**G.**
Gor. 23/5—6/6/36.**L.**
Gor. 4—25/12/37.**G.**
Gor. 7—28/10/39.**G.**
Gor. 6—31/1/42.**G.**
Gor. 10/2/44. *Not repaired.*

BOILERS:
1205.
1207 *(ex6097)* 11/5/07.
1214 *(ex6104)* 4/2/11.
 835 *(exB1 5195)* 22/11/13.
 498 *(new)* 9/10/20.
 801 *(new)* 8/10/27.
 128 *(exB1 5196)* 28/5/32.
 684 *(ex6099)* 3/6/33.
 922 *(ex6096)* 26/1/35.
  55 *(ex6097)* 25/4/36.
 684 *(ex6103)* 25/12/37.
 797 *(ex6103)* 28/10/39.

SHEDS:
Sheffield 8/12/22.
Mexborough ?/?
Doncaster 2/6/24.
Gorton 19/2/25.
New England 16/5/25.
Copley Hill 19/1/26.
Neasden 24/10/32.
Immingham 15/12/32.
March 9/5/33.
Lincoln 11/9/35.
Immingham 7/7/37.
Lincoln 2/9/37.
Gorton 28/10/39.
Lincoln 29/10/39.
Langwith Jct. 16/8/42.
Doncaster 21/11/42.
Langwith Jct. 29/11/42.
Ardsley 20/2/43.

RENUMBERED:
6095 21/2/25.

WITHDRAWN: 3/7/39.
CME order No.953 for repair
issued 11/9/39.

CONDEMNED: 10/2/44.
Cut up at Gorton.

6096

Beyer, Peacock 4817.

To traffic 6/1906.

REPAIRS:
Gor. 13/1—3/3/11.**G.**
Gor. 4/5—4/7/14.**G.**
Gor. 29/5—7/8/15.**G.**
Gor. 8/5—3/7/20.**G.**
Gor. 19/8—21/10/22.**G.**
Gor. 1/3—26/4/24.**G.**
Gor. 27/8—19/11/27.**G.**
Superheated boiler fitted.
Gor. 14/12/29—25/1/30.**G.**
Gor. 26/7—16/8/30.**G.**
New 19in S.V. cylinders fitted.
Gor. 23/7—13/8/32.**G.**
Gor. 18/8—15/9/34.**G.**
Gor. 17—31/10/36.**G.**
Gor. 23/4—21/5/38.**G.**
Gor. 16—30/11/40.**G.**
Gor. 25/9—17/10/42.**G.**
Gor. 16/6—21/7/45.**G.**
Gor. 26/10—2/11/46.**L.**
Gor. 4/7/47. *Not repaired.*

BOILERS:
1206.
1207 *(ex6095)* 3/3/11.
1214 *(ex6095)* 4/7/14.
 834 *(ex6099)* 7/8/15.
1434 *(new)* 3/7/20.
 802 *(new)* 19/11/27.
 922 *(ex6098)* 13/8/32.
 132 *(ex6104)* 15/9/34.
 681 *(ex6104)* 31/10/36.
 923 *(ex6097)* 30/11/40.
 127 *(ex6101)* 17/10/42.
  55 *(ex6101)* 21/7/45.

SHEDS:
Sheffield 8/12/22.
New England 29/5/25.
Copley Hill 20/1/26.
Lincoln 8/7/39.
Langwith Jct. 9/8/42.
Lincoln 16/8/42.

RENUMBERED:
6096 26/4/24.
1481 7/9/46.

CONDEMNED: 4/7/47.
Cut up at Gorton.

6097

IMMINGHAM

Beyer, Peacock 4818.

To traffic 6/1906.

REPAIRS:
Gor. 6—27/4/07.**G.**
Gor. 3/7—21/8/15.**G.**
Gor. 24/4—3/7/20.**G.**
Gor. 6/5—29/7/22.**G.**
Gor. 21/6—27/12/24.**G.**
Gor. 6—13/6/25.**L.**
Gor. 27/2—22/5/26.**G.**
Superheated boiler fitted.
Gor. 12/5—7/7/28.**G.**
Gor. 14/2—14/3/31.**G.**
Gor. 27/8—24/9/32.**G.**
Gor. 28/10—9/12/33.**G.**
Gor. 10—24/8/35.**G.**
Gor. 15/5—5/6/37.**G.**
Gor. 20/7—10/8/40.**G.**
Gor. 19/4—10/5/41.**H.**
New cylinders fitted.
Gor. 30/9—17/10/42.**G.**
Gor. 28/10—11/11/44.**G.**
Gor. 22/2—29/3/47.**G.**
Painted green.

BOILERS:
1207.
1205 *(ex6095)* 27/4/07.
1209 *(ex6102)* 21/8/15.
1333 *(new)* 3/7/20.
 539 *(ex6100)* 27/12/24.
 684 *(new)* 22/5/26.
 132 *(new)* 14/3/31.
 802 *(ex6096)* 24/9/32.
  55 *(ex6102)* 9/12/33.
 923 *(ex6099)* 24/8/35.
 802 *(exB1 5195)* 10/8/40.
 132 *(ex6100)* 17/10/42.
 922 *(ex6098)* 11/11/44.
3265 *(exO4 6347)* 29/3/47.

SHEDS:
Sheffield 27/10/22.
Mexborough ?/?
Doncaster 28/3/24.
Ardsley 3/1/25.
Doncaster 23/9/32.
Mexborough 25/1/33.

Copley Hill 8/3/33.
Lincoln 12/8/39.
Ardsley 11/7/47.

RENUMBERED:
6097 27/12/24.
1482 12/1/47.

CONDEMNED: 24/11/50.
Into Gor. for cut up 25/11/50.

6098

Beyer, Peacock 4819.

To traffic 6/1906.

REPAIRS:
Gor. 8/7—29/10/10.**G.**
Gor. 29/7—23/12/16.**G.**
Gor. 14/1—10/6/22.**G.**
Ross 'pops' fitted.
Gor. 30/8/24—3/1/25.**G.**
Gor. 11/7—5/9/25.**G.**
Gor. 20/11/26—5/2/27.**G.**
Gor. 18/8—6/10/28.**G.**
Superheated boiler fitted.
Gor. 11/10—15/11/30.**G.**
Gor. 18/6—9/7/32.**G.**
Gor. 7/7—18/8/34.**G.**
21in P.V. cylinders fitted.
Gor. 28/11—19/12/36.**G.**
Gor. 8—29/1/38.**G.**
Gor. 21/8—20/9/41.**G.**
Gor. 21/9—9/10/43.**G.**
Gor. 27/9—7/10/44.**L.**
Gor. 19—26/5/45.**L.**
Gor. 25/8—29/9/45.**G.**
Gor. 22/12/45—19/1/46.**L.**
After derailment.
Gor. 26/9/49. *Not repaired.*

BOILERS:
1208.
1210 *(ex6100)* 29/10/10.
1214 *(ex6096)* 23/12/16.
1333 *(ex6097)* 3/1/25.
 922 *(new)* 6/10/28.
 801 *(ex6095)* 9/7/32.
 132 *(ex6096)* 19/12/36.
  55 *(ex6095)* 29/1/38.
 922 *(exB1 5196)* 20/9/41.
 128 *(ex6103)* 9/10/43.
 127 *(ex6096)* 29/9/45.

SHEDS:
Sheffield 6/10/22.
Mexborough ?/?
Doncaster 2/6/24.
Copley Hill 10/1/25.
Ardsley 25/1/40.

Nos.6096 to 6102 retained 19in. cylinders and slide valves when the superheater was put in, and 6096, 6097, 6099 and 6102 retained this size, and type to withdrawal. A pair of new 19in. cylinders was put into 6096 in August 1930 and into 6097 in May 1941 whilst a new right hand cylinder was put on 6099 in February 1941, and on 6102 in March 1943.

(above) Subsequent to superheating, a change to 21in. cylinders and piston valves took place on 6101 (June 1927), 6100 (May 1932) and 6098 (August 1934).

(left) The original Robinson shapely chimney was retained at least to 1928 although change had been taking place for three years. The fitting of superheater was accompanied by a smokebox ash ejector with the steam pipe entering at the front end. Nottingham (Victoria).

In April 1925, a 'plant pot' chimney only 1ft 3in. high was put on 6101, although this was clearly not to bring the engine within the 13ft 0in. load gauge as the height to the top of the dome was still 13ft 3¹⁵⁄₁₆in. and the whistle remained above the cab roof. This N7 type chimney was taken off during the March/June 1927 shopping.

During 1925 to 1928, all ten were changed to a plain taper chimney although the height to the top was still 13ft 2¼in.

From 1935 the plain taper chimney was also supplanted by a shaped type giving a height to top of 12ft 10¾in. and all duly acquired this type and had it at withdrawal. During the middle 1920's the Ramsbottom safety valves were replaced by two Ross 'pops' usually without any cover around their base. March shed.

6098 continued.
Copley Hill 3/11/46.
Ardsley 16/2/47.

RENUMBERED:
6098 3/1/25.
1483 12/1/47.

CONDEMNED: 26/9/49.
Cut up at Dukinfield.

6099

Beyer, Peacock 4820.

To traffic 6/1906.

REPAIRS:
Gor. 14/10—26/11/10.**G.**
Gor. 3/5—14/6/13.**G.**
Gor. 12/9—31/10/14.**G.**
Gor. 12/2—30/4/21.**G.**
Gor. 12/8—14/10/22.**G.**
Gor. 1/3—26/4/24.**G.**
Gor. 12/6—11/12/26.**G.**
Superheated boiler & new S.V.
cylinders fitted.
Gor. 27/4—15/6/29.**G.**
Gor. 12—19/4/30.**L.**
Gor. 28/3—2/5/31.**G.**
Gor. 25/3—8/4/33.**G.**
Gor. 27/4—11/5/35.**G.**
Gor. 12—31/12/36.**G.**
Gor. 30/3—27/4/40.**G.**
Gor. 25/1—8/2/41.**L.**
New R.H. cylinder.
Gor. 1—12/6/43.**G.**
Gor. 11/11—9/12/44.**G.**
Gor. 31/8/46.**L.**

BOILERS:
1209.
1208 *(ex6098)* 26/11/10.
  834 *(ex6104)* 14/6/13.
1211 *(ex6103)* 31/10/14.
1149 *(new)* 30/4/21.
1210 *(exB1 5196)* 26/4/24.
  784 *(new)* 11/12/26.
  684 *(ex6097)* 2/5/31.
  923 *(ex6104)* 8/4/33.
  797 *(exB1 5196)* 11/5/35.
  801 *(ex6098)* 31/12/36.
  122 *(ex6104)* 27/4/40.
  801 *(ex6100)* 12/6/43.
  684 *(ex6102)* 9/12/44.

SHEDS:
Gorton 30/9/21.
Sheffield ?/?
New England 30/5/25.
Ardsley 2/1/26.
Copley Hill *by* 1/35.
Gorton 25/1/40.
Ardsley 27/4/40.
Doncaster 21/11/42.
Copley Hill 25/6/45.
Bradford 2/12/45.
Ardsley 19/5/46.

RENUMBERED:
6099 26/4/24.
1484 31/8/46

CONDEMNED: 20/11/47.
Cut up at Dukinfield.

6100

Beyer, Peacock 4821.

To traffic 6/1906.

REPAIRS:
Gor. 2/11—25/12/09.**G.**
Gor. 25/4—30/5/14.**G.**
Gor. 29/7—9/9/16.**G.**
Gor. 26/6—31/7/20.**G.**
Gor. 22/7—23/9/22.**G.**
Gor. 23/8—8/11/24.**G.**
Gor. 30/5/25—9/1/26.**G.**
Superheater fitted.
Gor. 23/6—4/8/28.**G.**
Gor. 18/1—1/3/30.**G.**
Gor. 26/3—7/5/32.**G.**
New 21in. P.V. cylinders fitted.
Gor. 2/6—23/6/34.**G.**
Heater connection fitted at front
end.
Gor. 10—31/10/36.**G.**
Gor. 18/6—2/7/38.**G.**
Gor. 3—17/8/40.**G.**
Gor. 5—27/3/43.**G.**
Gor. 13/10—10/11/45.**H.**

BOILERS:
1210.

833 *(new)* 25/12/09.
836 *(ex6104)* 30/5/14.
1205 *(ex6097)* 9/9/16.
  539 *(new)* 31/7/20.
1149 *(ex6099)* 8/11/24.
  681 *(exB1 5195)* 1/3/30.
  802 *(ex6097)* 23/6/34.
  127 *(ex6101)* 31/10/36.
  132 *(ex6098)* 2/7/38.
  801 *(ex6099)* 17/8/40.
  802 *(ex6097)* 27/3/43.
  923 *(ex6104)* 10/11/45.

SHEDS:
Sheffield 8/12/22.
March 4/6/23.
Mexborough 10/23.
Doncaster 2/6/24.
Copley Hill 19/11/24.
Ardsley 25/1/40.
Copley Hill 19/10/41.
Ardsley 6/9/42.

RENUMBERED:
6100 8/11/24.
1485 22/9/46.

CONDEMNED: 4/6/49.
Cut up at Dukinfield.

Only on 6101 and 6098 (*see* previous page, middle) was there a cover to the base of the valves, and on 6098 shorter and larger diameter valves were used. This 1934 photograph shows a new boiler with a low dome, fitted in December 1933, but the chimney is still over 13ft 0in. Note the board on the front of the tender to increase coal capacity for a long distance excursion being run by the *Bradford Telegraph & Argus* newspaper. Bradford (Bowling/ Hammerton St.) shed.

Until at least 1935 there were no side screens on the cab sides. Side screens were fitted to 6097 in June 1937. Note that the chimney is now below 13ft 0in. but on the boiler carried from August 1935 to July 1940 the dome height exceeded 13ft 0in. In August 1940 No.6097 was the last of the ten engines to be brought within the Group Standard load gauge. Brunswick shed.

No.6100 was under 13ft 0in. from July 1938. It was the only one noted with oval heads to the buffers, round heads being standard for the class. At its July 1938 shopping the classification was put on the front buffer beam, this having been introduced in March 1938.

Some time after 1940, No.1482 (as 6097) was fitted with Group Standard front buffers, the only one of the class so equipped. It was also unusual in having the lamp iron removed from the top of the smokebox and in having the wheel changed to a second handle for the smokebox door fastening. Ardsley shed, June 1950.

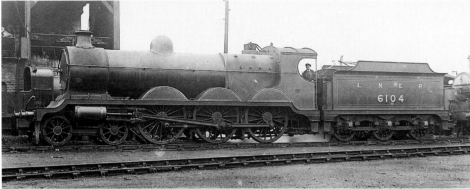

Lubrication throughout was by sight feed and until the middle 1920's was not to be discerned. Until September 1927 all ten retained their original tender, which had solid coping plates from building. Bradford shed.

With superheating either Detroit or Eureka sight feed lubrication was used, and none got a mechanical type. On the first one superheated (*see* page 57, top) the pipes from the cab were tidily arranged. This standard progressively deteriorated as the view of No.6100 on the previous page shows. In October 1927 No.6095 (*see* page 54, middle) and in November 1928 No.6104, were coupled with tenders from early C4 class engines Nos.5265 and 5264 which still had open coal rails.

By 1938 both these tenders had been altered to plated coping but No.6104 had another tender change in December 1943. Note that the lamp iron on top of the smokebox is still there but a GS type has been added on the smokebox door. The tender coping plate has been fitted on to the face of the coal rails, the give-away being the absence of beading around the edge. No.6095's tender remained with it to withdrawal in February 1944. It then served with J11 and O4 class engines to November 1962. Lincoln (GC) shed, 1938.

6101

Beyer, Peacock 4822.

To traffic 6/1906.

REPAIRS:
Gor. 10/2—17/6/11.**G.**
Gor. 6/7—16/8/19.**G.**
Gor. 30/4—18/6/21.**G.**
Gor. 16/12/22—3/3/23.**G.**
Gor. 1/11—25/4/25.**G.**
Superheated boiler fitted.
Gor. 26/3—25/6/27.**G.**
New 21in P.V. cylinders ftted.
Gor. 17/11/28—19/1/29.**G.**
Gor. 11/7—8/9/31.**G.**
Gor. 4—18/3/33.**L.**
Gor. 25/11—16/12/33.**G.**
Gor. 7—28/3/36.**G.**
Altered to 13ft 0in gauge.
Gor. 3/9—15/10/38.**G.**
Gor. 25/3—11/4/42.**G.**
Gor. 12—27/3/43.**L.**
Gor. 16—30/12/44.**G.**

BOILERS:
1211.
1212 *(ex6102)* 17/6/11.
1141 *(new)* 16/8/19.
1470 *(new)* 25/4/25.
 122 *(exB1 5196)* 25/6/27.
 784 *(ex6099)* 8/9/31.
 127 *(new)* 16/12/33.
 121 *(ex6102)* 28/3/36.
 127 *(ex6100)* 15/10/38.
 55 *(ex6098)* 11/4/42.
 132 *(ex6097)* 30/12/44.

SHEDS:
Sheffield 19/5/22.
March 6/23.
Mexborough 10/23.
Doncaster 22/3/24.
Gorton 23/4/25.
Copley Hill 29/5/25.
Immingham 18/3/33.
Copley Hill 24/8/33.
Ardsley 25/1/40.
Bradford 11/7/41.
Copley Hill 10/12/42.
Ardsley 28/3/43.
Bradford 30/6/43.
Ardsley 7/7/43.
Bradford 2/12/45.
Ardsley 19/5/46.

RENUMBERED:
6101 25/4/25.
1486 1/12/46.

CONDEMNED: 7/10/47.
Into Gor. for cut up 11/10/47 but cut up at Dukinfield.

6102

Beyer, Peacock 4823.

To traffic 6/1906

REPAIRS:
Gor. 9/12/10—17/2/11.**G.**
Gor. 12/9—19/12/14.**G.**
Gor. 9/7—6/8/21.**G**
Gor. 13/1—3/3/23.**G.**
Gor. 29/11/24—7/2/25.**G.**
Gor. 7/5—17/9/27.**G.**
Superheated boiler fitted.
Gor. 28/9—9/11/29.**G.**
Gor. 17/10—21/11/31.**G.**
Gor. 3—24/9/32.**G.**
Gor. 12/8—2/9/33.**G.**
Gor. 18/1—8/2/36.**G.**
Altered to 13ft 0in gauge.
Gor. 26/12/36—23/1/37.**L.**
Gor. 25/12/37—8/1/38.**L.**
Gor. 4—25/2/39.**G.**
Gor. 10/2—6/3/43.**G.**
New R.H. cylinder fitted.
Gor. 5—30/9/44.**G.**

BOILERS:
1212.
1209 *(ex6099)* 17/2/11.
 833 *(ex6100)* 19/12/14.
1182 *(new)* 6/8/21.
 798 *(new)* 17/9/27.
 55 *(exB1 5195)* 21/11/31.
 121 *(new)* 2/9/33.
 128 *(ex6103)* 8/2/36.
 121 *(ex6101)* 25/2/39.
 684 *(ex6104)* 6/3/43.
 681 *(exB1 5195)* 30/9/44.

SHEDS:
Sheffield 19/5/22.
March 6/23.
Sheffield ?/?
New England 27/4/25.
Copley Hill 26/10/25.
Gorton 25/1/40.
Ardsley 28/2/40.
Bradford 2/12/45.
Ardsley 19/5/46.

RENUMBERED:
6102 7/2/25.
1487 12/1/47.

CONDEMNED: 10/12/47.
Into Gor. for cut up 13/12/47 but cut up at Dukinfield.

6103

Beyer, Peacock 4824.

To traffic 7/1906.

REPAIRS:
Gor. 28/4—8/7/11.**G.**
Gor. 25/7—26/9/14.**G.**
Gor. 18/1—22/11/19.**G.**
Gor. 9/4—4/6/21.**G.**
Gor. 17/2—23/6/23.**G.**
Gor. 13/9—29/11/24.**G.**
Gor. 2/1—13/3/26.**G.**
Gor. 8/1—21/5/27.**G.**
Superheated boiler & new 21in P.V. cylinders fitted.
Gor. 8/12/28—9/2/29.**G.**
Gor. 22/11/30—10/1/31.**G.**
Gor. 9—30/4/32.**L.**
Gor. 17/6—8/7/33.**G.**
Gor. 28/10—11/11/33.**L.**
Gor. 16/3—6/4/35.**G.**
Gor. 23/1—13/2/37.**G.**
Gor. 18/2—11/3/39.**G.**
Gor. 12/6—12/7/41.**G.**
Gor. 8/6—10/7/43.**G.**
New cylinders fitted.
Gor. 18/5—14/9/46.**G.**

BOILERS:
1213.
1211 *(ex6101)* 8/7/11.
1207 *(ex6096)* 26/9/14.
1142 *(new)* 22/11/19.
 833 *(exB1 5195)* 13/3/26.
1470 *(ex6101)* 21/5/27.
 797 *(exB1 5196)* 10/1/31.
 128 *(ex6095)* 8/7/33.
 684 *(ex6095)* 6/4/35.
 797 *(ex6099)* 13/2/37.
 128 *(ex6102)* 11/3/39.
 122 *(ex6099)* 10/7/43.
3395 *(exO4 6511)* 14/9/46.

SHEDS:
Sheffield 19/5/22.
Copley Hill 27/5/25.
Doncaster 21/9/32.
Mexborough 30/1/33.
Immingham 16/3/33.
March 3/6/33.
Lincoln 8/7/35.
Retford 26/6/39.
Lincoln 15/3/40.
Doncaster 29/11/42.
Copley Hill 25/6/45.
Ardsley 16/2/47.

RENUMBERED:
1103c *after 4/8/23 at shed.*
6103 29/11/24.
1488 17/11/46.

CONDEMNED: 7/10/48.
Into Gor. for cut up 9/10/48 but cut up at Dukinfield.

6104

Beyer, Peacock 4825.

To traffic 7/1906.

REPAIRS:
Gor. 26/3—9/7/10.**G.**
Gor. 9/3—15/6/12.**G.**
Gor. 7/2—7/3/14.**G.**
Gor. 6/8—19/11/21.**G.**
Gor. 17/5—26/7/24.**G.**
Gor. 5/12/25—20/2/26.**G.**
Gor. 2/10/26—12/3/27.**G.**
Superheater & new 21in P.V. cylinders fitted.
Gor. 22/9—10/11/28.**G.**
Gor. 20/12/30—24/1/31.**G.**
Gor. 22/10—26/11/32.**G.**
Gor. 14/7—4/8/34.**G.**
Gor. 18/4—9/5/36.**G.**
Gor. 15/1—12/2/38.**G.**
Gor. 16/3—13/4/40.**G.**
Gor. 15/1—6/2/43.**G.**
Gor. 4—5/2/44.**L.**
Tender only repair.
Gor. 23/12/44—20/1/45.**G.**
Gor. 4/7/47. *Not repaired.*

BOILERS:
1214.
 834 *(new)* 9/7/10.
 836 *(exB1 5196)* 15/6/12.
1208 *(ex6099)* 7/3/14.
 55 *(new)* 26/7/24.
 923 *(new)* 10/11/28.
 132 *(ex6097)* 26/11/32.
 681 *(ex6100)* 4/8/34.
 922 *(ex6095)* 9/5/36.
 122 *(exB1 5196)* 12/2/38.
 684 *(ex6095)* 13/4/40.
 923 *(ex6096)* 6/2/43.
 801 *(ex6099)* 20/1/45.

SHEDS:
Sheffield 15/4/22.
March 6/23.
Mexborough 10/23.
Sheffield 12/8/24.
Copley Hill 27/5/25.
March 9/5/33.
Lincoln 3/10/35.
Immingham 6/7/37.
Lincoln 3/9/37.

RENUMBERED:
6104 26/7/24.
1489 12/1/47.

CONDEMNED: 4/7/47.
Cut up at Gorton.

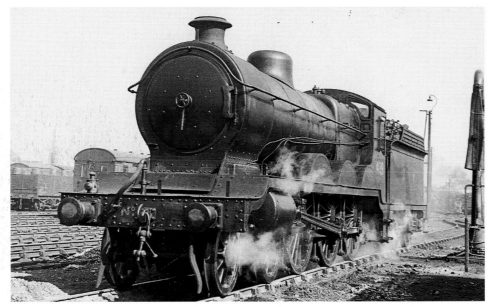

In December 1943 No.6104 (1489 from January 1947) was changed to tender No.5180 which was a spare. This had served B5 class No.5180 until October 1924 and its original open coal rails had been plated on the inside - it was cut-up with 1485. No.6104 (1489) was last repaired in January 1945. Note the use of snaphead instead of the normal countersunk rivets for the smokebox door baffle plate and the front buffer beam. Lincoln (GN) shed, April 1947.

Four of the class, Nos.6096, 6097, 6098 and 6100 ran for varying periods with a tender built for a J11 class engine. As these were also the standard 4000 gallon type, no difference was discernible, because they also had water pick-up apparatus. Note the low dome on a boiler new in May 1930. Woodford shed, 1935.

During the war, and in the process of conforming to the 13ft 0in. composite load gauge, Gorton altered some of the tall dome covers to a flat top which gave a peculiar angular look to them. They were no guide to the size of the dome itself because No.1486 had the same boiler as No.6096 in the illustration above.

Unlike many other classes, B4 engines retained the wheel and handle for smokebox door fastening, with the sole exception of green painted engine No.1482 (see page 60, top). Note the wartime use of snaphead rivets for the smokebox wrapper plate to save on labour.

Although the Great Central had painted them black, the LNER regarded B4 as a passenger class with coupled wheels big enough to qualify for green lined livery. Nos.1101 and 1102 both ex paint shop 28th April 1923 were the first to be green and they got L.&N.E.R. but retained their GC large brass number plates. Note pipe for ash ejector as compared with on a superheated engine (*see* page 56, bottom). Removal of the GC plate and change to LNER 6102 was on 7th February 1925. The similar change to 6101 was on 25th April 1925.

(*above*) The next one, ex paint shop 4th August 1923, was given the same treatment except for omission of ampersand and full points, only LNER being used. Later, the regional suffix C was put on by the home shed. Note absence of a cover around the Ramsbottom safety valves. 6103 lost its GC number plate and got tender 1103 changed to 6103 on 29th November 1924. Sheffield Neepsend shed, July 1924.

(*right*) The next two to get the LNER number were 6096 and 6099, both ex works 26th April 1924. Large brass number plates carrying 6096 and 6099 were fitted with the letter C painted above them, otherwise they were unpainted and remained in Great Central black livery. LNER green was only applied to 6099 in December 1926 and to 6096 in November 1927.

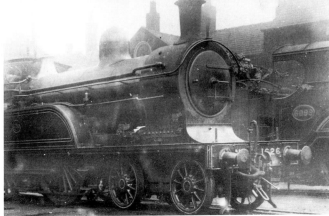

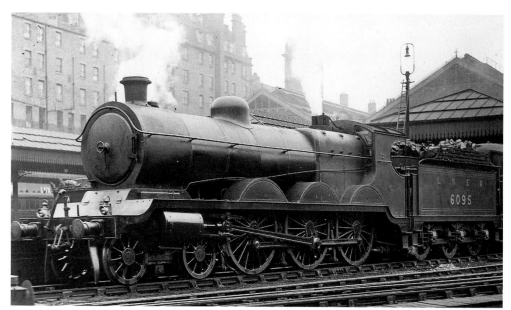

(left) The other five went straight to LNER standard green livery and numbering, 6104 (26th July 1924), 6100 (8th November 1924), 6097 (27th December 1924), 6098 (3rd January 1925) and 6095 (21st February 1925). Nottingham (Victoria).

(below) Between November 1929 (6102) and September 1931 (6101) all had the number moved from tender to cab. They continued in green and 6098 to works on 21st September 1943 was the last to wear it. Doncaster shed, August 1932.

From November 1941 all went into unlined black painting and from July 1942 with only NE on the tender. No.6095 ex works on 31st January 1942 would have LNER on its tender and be withdrawn as such on 10th February 1944. The other nine duly got NE in shaded block transfers. Amersham, March 1946.

Engines having heavy repair from January 1946 got LNER restored by transfers onto black painting but only two B4 were so treated, 6098 (19th January 1946) and 6103 (14th September 1946). They were renumbered 1483 (*see* page 62, bottom) on 12th January 1947, and 1488 on 17th November 1946 at Leeds Copley Hill shed by local painters. Although this engine had been No.6103 it had been coupled with tender 6104 since 9th February 1929 which explains the number chalked on it. Dukinfield works, October 1948.

Only 6097, renumbered 1482 on 12th January 1947, had green livery restored. From a general repair on 22nd February to 29th March 1947 it came out in green, fully lined, but with yellow painted and unshaded numbers in Gill sans characters and retained this style to withdrawal on 24th November 1950. Ardsley shed, June 1950.

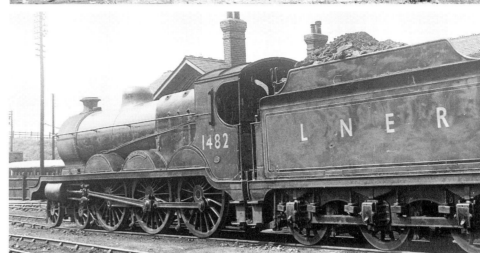

(*above*) Only delivered in June 1906, No.1097 was used on 12th July 1906 to haul the train used by guests and management attending the cutting of the first sod for the big new dock at Immingham. Thereafter, until 1950 it carried the name IMMINGHAM. The illustrations on pages 54 and above show the name as carried and flush with the top of the splashers. The larger letters displayed above the splasher are almost certainly just a re-touching of the official photograph to give clearer reproduction in the press.

(*right*) No.1484 was withdrawn on 20th November 1947 and here on 11th March 1948 is at Dukinfield where it was cut up.

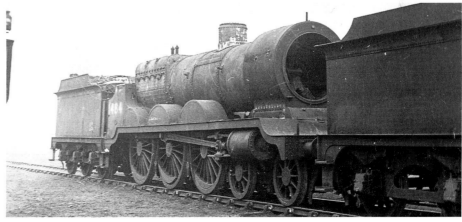

Eight further engines, Nos.180 to 187, were built by Beyer, Peacock in 1904. At Grouping Nos.181, 183 and 186 had got J11 tenders with solid coping, 180 and 184 still had their original tenders with open coal rails (*see* page 68, top) whilst 182, 185 and 187 had railed tenders from D9 class. Note that the casing to the Ramsbottom safety valves has been taken off. Guide Bridge.

Although superheating of the class began in June 1923, No.6070 was not so equipped until May 1936.

CLASS B 5

6067

Neilson Reid 6235.

To traffic 11/1902.

REPAIRS:
Gor. ?/?—11/07.**G**.
Gor. 28/10/11—6/1/12.**G**.
Gor. 1/3—22/11/19.**G**.
Gor. 22/10/21—11/3/22.**G**.
Gor. 23/8—25/10/24.**G**.
Gor. 31/7—6/11/26.**G**.
Gor. 21/7—15/9/28.**G**.
Superheated boiler fitted.
Gor. 21/6—23/8/30.**G**.
21in type 8K cylinders fitted.
Gor. 9/4—7/5/32.**G**.
Gor. 25/11—16/12/33.**G**.
Gor. 2—16/11/35.**G**.
Gor. 27/11—18/12/37.**G**.
Gor. 3—24/8/40.**G**.
Gor. 17/8—5/9/42.**G**.
Gor. 16/12/44—20/1/45.**G**.
Gor. 31/8/46.**L**.

BOILERS:
338.
1288 *(new)* 11/07.
338 *(ex5183)* 6/1/12.
827 *(exB9 6112)* 22/11/19.
1772 *(ex5187)* 25/10/24.
905 *(new)* 15/9/28.
848 *(ex5185)* 7/5/32.
893 *(ex5187)* 16/12/33.
148 *(exQ4 5057)* 16/11/35.
725 *(exB9 6107)* 18/12/37.
3736 *(new)* 5/9/42.
837 *(ex5183)* 20/1/45.

SHEDS:
Mexborough 19/5/22.
Doncaster 2/6/24.
Lincoln 18/11/26.
Sheffield 15/11/35.
Mexborough 31/5/43.

RENUMBERED:
6067 25/10/24.
1678 10/11/46

CONDEMNED: 20/11/47.
Cut up at Dukinfield.

6068

Neilson Reid 6236.

To traffic 11/1902.

REPAIRS:
Gor. 18/5—13/7/07.**G**.
Gor. 15/2—5/4/13.**G**.
Gor. 24/5—13/3/20.**G**.
Gor. 3/9—26/11/21.**G**.
Gor. 24/3—14/7/23.**G**.
Gor. 29/8/25—9/1/26.**G**.
Superheated boiler fitted.
Gor. 29/10—24/12/27.**G**.
New R.H. cylinder fitted.
Gor. 3/5—14/6/30.**G**.
Gor. 19/12/30—23/1/32.**G**.
Gor. 2—23/12/33.**G**.
Gor. 15/6—6/7/35.**G**.
Gor. 28/8—2/10/37.**G**.
Gor. 17—24/12/38.**L**.
Gor. 25/5—8/6/40.**G**.
Gor. 2—26/6/43.**G**.
New L.H. cylinder fitted.
Gor. 12/1—2/2/46.**G**.
Gor. 13—27/9/47.**L**.
After collision.

BOILERS:
339.
342 *(ex6071)* 13/7/07.
340 *(ex5180)* 5/4/13.
1842 *(new)* 13/3/20.
642 *(new)* 9/1/26.
407 *(exQ4 6180)* 14/6/30.
642 *(ex5187)* 23/1/32.
833 *(new)* 23/12/33.
1912 *(ex5185)* 6/7/35.
333 *(exQ4 5039)* 2/10/37.
138 *(exQ4 5064)* 26/6/43.
722 *(ex5180)* 2/2/46.

SHEDS:
Mexborough 19/1/17.
Ardsley 5/1/24.
Immingham 22/5/24.
Copley Hill 22/2/26.
Immingham 27/4/26.
Doncaster 26/7/27.
Woodford 14/7/28.
Sheffield 30/3/36.
Trafford Park 6/10/46.
Mexborough 24/8/47.

RENUMBERED:
6068 9/1/26.

1679 7/7/46.

CONDEMNED: 23/12/47.
Into Gor. for cut up 27/12/47
but cut up at Dukinfield.

6069

Neilson Reid 6237.

To traffic 11/1902.

REPAIRS:
Gor. 9/11—14/12/07.**G**.
Gor. 6/3—24/4/09.**G**.
Gor. 11/5—29/6/12.**G**.
Gor. 4/12/15—12/2/16.**G**.
Gor. 21/8—13/11/20.**G**.
Gor. 14/10—23/12/22.**G**.
Gor. 28/2—30/5/25.**G**.
Gor. 20/11/26—12/2/27.**G**.
Gor. 15/12/28—9/2/29.**G**.
Gor. 20/9—1/11/30.**G**.
Gor. 17/12/32—14/1/33.**G**.
Superheated boiler fitted.
Gor. 22/9—6/10/34.**G**.
Gor. 16—30/5/36.**G**.
Gor. 8/10—5/11/38.**G**.
New cylinders fitted.
Gor. 29/6—27/7/40.**G**.
Gor. 18/5—13/6/42.**L**.
New L.H. cylinder fitted.
Gor. 13—28/8/43.**G**.
Gor. 27/7—24/8/46.**G**.
Gor. 13/11/48. *Not repaired.*

BOILERS:
340.
832 *(ex5187)* 14/12/07.
341 *(ex6070)* 24/4/09.
1288 *(ex6067)* 29/6/12.
826 *(ex5181)* 12/2/16.
26 *(new)* 13/11/20.
1796 *(ex6070)* 12/2/27.
1844 *(ex5187)* 1/11/30.
370 *(exQ4 6178)* 14/1/33.
553 *(exQ4 6133)* 6/10/34.
722 *(exQ4 5058)* 30/5/36.
148 *(ex6067)* 5/11/38.
874 *(ex5187)* 27/7/40.
148 *(ex5187)* 28/8/43.

SHEDS:
Mexborough 1/9/22.
Doncaster 22/3/24.
Lincoln 10/6/25.
Sheffield 30/5/36.

Trafford Park 6/10/46.
Heaton Mersey 8/1/47.
Mexborough 24/8/47.

RENUMBERED:
6069 30/5/25.
1680 24/8/46.

CONDEMNED: 13/11/48.
Cut up at Dukinfield.

6070

Neilson Reid 6238.

To traffic 11/1902.

REPAIRS:
Gor. 5/10—13/11/09.**G**.
Gor. 31/5—20/9/13.**G**.
Gor. 31/3—23/6/17.**G**.
Gor. 8/10/21—14/1/22.**G**.
Gor. 23/2—19/4/24.**G**.
Gor. 17/4—7/8/26.**G**.
Gor. 10/11—22/12/28.**G**.
Gor. 2/5—6/6/31.**G**.
Gor. 2/12/33—20/1/34.**G**.
Gor. 4/4—2/5/36.**G**.
Superheated boiler fitted.
Gor. 13/2—13/3/37.**G**.
Gor. 4/2/39. *Not repaired.*

BOILERS:
341.
828 *(ex5183)* 13/11/09.
342 *(ex6068)* 20/9/13.
830 *(ex5184)* 23/6/17.
1796 *(ex5186)* 19/4/24.
1842 *(ex6068)* 7/8/26.
26 *(ex5181)* 6/6/31.
468A *(exQ4 5152)* 20/1/34.
911 *(ex5181)* 2/5/36.

SHEDS:
Mexborough *at* 5/22.
Lincoln 30/6/31.
Immingham 21/7/31.
Lincoln 7/7/37.
Immingham 2/9/37.
Lincoln 16/5/38.

RENUMBERED:
6070 19/4/24.

CONDEMNED: 6/3/39.
Cut up at Gorton.

WORKS CODES:- Cw - Cowlairs. Dar- Darlington. Don - Doncaster. Ghd - Gateshead. Gor - Gorton. Inv - Inverurie. Str - Stratford.
REPAIR CODES:- **C/H** - Casual Heavy. **C/L** - Casual Light. **G** - General. **H**- Heavy. **H/I** - Heavy Intermediate. **L** - Light. **L/I** - Light Intermediate. **N/C** - Non-Classified.

The intention to equip B5 with a larger and superheated boiler arose in very early LNER days and the first evidence was No.184, ex paint shop on 28th July 1923. It had an O4 class boiler, 3in. bigger than its original, and the cab had double windows with a rear extension to its roof. No others were rebuilt in this manner. Note the original tender was retained, but the large brass cab number plate was superseded by the LNER type. Gorton shed.

(*left*) Between January 1926 (6068) and May 1936 all fourteen were rebuilt with a superheated boiler of the same diameter as the original but as used on Q4 class. Its deeper firebox needed it to be pitched 7in. higher with the consequent shorter chimney and lower dome, also change to 'pop' safety valves. All had Gresley anti-vacuum valve behind the chimney. The cab front was altered to a single window and only at the side of the firebox. In December 1927 the first rebuild with the O4 boiler No.5184, was brought into line with the others by changing it to a Q4 boiler and an ordinary cab. Although the tender still has open coal rails it is not the original but one from a D9 class which it had from January 1924 to January 1940. Gorton shed, July 1931.

When the higher pitched Q4 Diagram 17 boiler was fitted, a 1ft 3in. plant pot chimney was provided giving an overall height of 12ft 10¾in. In conjunction with a low dome boiler this brought the engine within the composite loading gauge. The shorter chimney was needed also on Nos.5183 and 6070, which at first ran with saturated Q4 boilers (*see* bottom illustration).

In September 1934, No.5186 was fitted with a cast chimney more in line with GC designs and all fourteen duly acquired this type which was also 1ft 3in. high. Doncaster shed, June 1935.

When Nos.5183 (in June 1929) and 6070 (in January 1934) first acquired Diagram 17 boilers, these were not superheated, having been built in March 1924 for Q4 class. The two B5's got superheated boilers from July 1935 (5183) and May 1936 (6070) (*see* page 72, top and page 78, second from top). This boiler served 5183 to May 1933. Grantham shed.

(*opposite, bottom*) The original chimney, and as fitted at Grouping, was a Robinson type 2ft 2¾in. high giving a total height from rail level of 13ft 3¹⁵⁄₁₆in. No.6067 is still without a superheater so the ash ejector is on the left hand side, but the steam supply pipe has been lengthened. Compare with illustration second from bottom on page 71. Gorton shed.

6071

Neilson Reid 6239.

To traffic 11/1902.

REPAIRS:
Gor. 8/12/06—16/2/07.**G.**
Gor. 1/11—6/12/13.**G.**
Gor. 7/5—5/11/21.**G.**
Gor. 30/6—15/9/23.**G.**
Gor. 2/5—11/7/25.**G.**
Gor. 24/12/27—17/3/28.**G.**
Superheated boiler fitted.
Gor. 1/2—8/3/30.**G.**
Gor. 9—23/7/32.**G.**
Gor. 7—21/7/34.**G.**
Gor. 25/1—15/2/36.**G.**
Gor. 15/5—19/6/37.**G.**
Gor. 16—23/9/39.**G.**
Gor. 3/12/42—2/1/43.**G.**
Gor. 19/10—7/12/46.**G.**

BOILERS:
342.
739 *(new)* 16/2/07.
831 *(ex5186)* 6/12/13.
165 *(new)* 5/11/21.
1901 *(ex6072)* 11/7/25.
899 *(new)* 17/3/28.
830 *(exB9 6105)* 23/7/32.
1842 *(exQ4 5071)* 21/7/34.
3723 *(new)* 15/2/36.
723 *(ex5182)* 23/9/39.
849 *(exQ4 6179)* 2/1/43.

SHEDS:
Mexborough 28/7/22.
Doncaster 26/2/24.
Immingham 18/7/25.
Woodford 18/7/28.
Gorton 24/7/39.
Mexborough 16/4/43.
Lincoln 22/12/46.
Mexborough 14/7/47.

RENUMBERED:
1071c 15/9/23.
6071 11/7/25.
1681 30/8/46.

CONDEMNED: 23/6/48.
Into Gor. for cut up 26/6/48 but cut up at Dukinfield.

6072

Neilson Reid 6240.

To traffic 11/1902.

REPAIRS:
Gor. 13—29/1/10.**G.**
Gor. 10/1—7/8/20.**G.**
Gor. 16/12/22—10/2/23.**G.**

Gor. 28/2—9/5/25.**G.**
Gor. 22/10—17/12/27.**G.**
Gor. 22/3—3/5/30.**G.**
Superheated boiler fitted.
Gor. 27/2—19/3/32.**G.**
Gor. 16—30/9/33.**G.**
Gor. 7/7—4/8/34.**L.**
Gor. 22/6—27/7/35.**G.**
21in type 8K cylinders fitted.
Gor. 28/5—18/6/38.**G.**
Gor. 10—24/2/40.**G.**
Gor. 14/11—5/12/42.**G.**
Gor. 3—21/10/44.**G.**

BOILERS:
343.
832 *(ex6069)* 29/1/10.
1901 *(new)* 7/8/20.
1770 *(ex5180)* 9/5/25.
336 *(exQ4 5139)* 3/5/30.
725 *(exB9 6110)* 19/3/32.
495 *(exQ4 6174)* 30/9/33.
833 *(ex6068)* 27/7/35.
910 *(exQ4 5137)* 18/6/38.
894 *(ex5184)* 24/2/40.
901 *(exB9 6113)* 5/12/42.
830 *(exQ4 6052)* 21/10/44.

SHEDS:
Mexborough 19/5/22.
Doncaster 19/5/24.
Lincoln 2/1/31.
Immingham 15/12/36.
Doncaster 15/3/40.
Mexborough 18/3/40.

RENUMBERED:
6072 9/5/25.
1682 1/9/46.

CONDEMNED: 14/8/47.
Cut up at Gorton.

5180

Beyer, Peacock 4531.

To traffic 1/1904,

REPAIRS:
Gor. 22/2—4/4/08.**G.**
Gor. 9/11—7/12/12.**G.**
Gor. 9/3/18—4/1/19.**G.**
Gor. 2/10—20/11/20.**G.**
Gor. 13/1—28/4/23.**G.**
Gor. 11/10—6/12/24.**G.**
Gor. 15/1—2/4/27.**G.**
Gor. 6/4—11/5/29.**G.**
Gor. 20/12/30—7/2/31.**G.**
Superheated boiler fitted.
Gor. 25/2—11/3/33.**G.**
Gor. 13—27/10/34.**G.**
Gor. 25/7—15/8/36.**G.**
Gor. 9/7—20/8/38.**G.**
21in type 8K cylinders fitted.

Gor. 2—30/11/40.**G.**
Gor. 23/8—4/9/43.**G.**
Gor. 6—27/10/45.**H.**
After collision.

BOILERS:
825.
340 *(ex6069)* 4/4/08.
1335 *(ex5187)* 7/12/12.
1770 *(new)* 4/1/19.
827 *(ex6067)* 6/12/24.
1891 *(ex5187)* 2/4/27.
728 *(exQ4 5162)* 7/2/31.
829 *(exQ4 5212)* 11/3/33.
901 *(ex5186)* 27/10/34.
1777 *(exQ4 5049)* 15/8/36.
640 *(ex5184)* 20/8/38.
722 *(exQ4 6136)* 4/9/43.
875 *(exQ4 5161)* 27/10/45.

SHEDS:
Immingham 19/5/22.
Doncaster 26/7/27.
Woodford 8/7/29.
Ardsley 30/7/30.
Woodford 21/8/30.
Mexborough 19/4/43.
Lincoln 29/12/46.
Mexborough 14/7/47.

RENUMBERED:
5180 6/12/24.
1683 12/5/46.

CONDEMNED: 23/12/47.
Into Gor. for cut up 27/12/47 but cut up at Dukinfield.

5181

Beyer, Peacock 4532.

To traffic 1/1904.

REPAIRS:
Gor. 18/1—18/4/08.**G.**
Gor. 20/3—15/5/09.**G.**
Gor. 17/4—10/7/15.**G.**
Gor. 25/12/20—12/3/21.**G.**
Gor. 5/5—21/7/23.**G.**
Gor. 15/8—28/11/25.**G.**
Gor. 30/7—24/9/27.**G.**
Gor. 9/3—13/4/29.**G.**
Gor. 31/1—28/2/31.**G.**
Gor. 26/11—31/12/32.**G.**
Superheated boiler fitted.
Gor. 2—16/6/34.**G.**
Gor. 21/3—11/4/36.**G.**
Gor. 23—30/5/36.**L.**
Gor. 1—29/5/37.**G.**
Gor. 22/10—19/11/38.**G.**
Gor. 22/2—22/3/41.**G.**
Gor. 5/7—2/8/41.**L.**
R.H. cylinder renewed.
Gor. 11/12/43—1/1/44.**G.**

Gor. 1/5/47. *Not repaired.*

BOILERS:
826.
830 *(ex5185)* 18/4/08.
826 *(ex spare)* 15/5/09.
341 *(ex5182)* 10/7/15.
826 *(ex6069)* 12/3/21.
26 *(ex6069)* 24/9/27.
1891 *(ex5180)* 28/2/31.
849 *(exQ4 6138)* 31/12/32.
911 *(exQ4 5957)* 16/6/34.
1842 *(exQ4 6071)* 11/4/36.
495 *(ex5187)* 19/11/38.
3729 *(new)* 22/3/41.
874 *(ex6069)* 1/1/44.

SHEDS:
Immingham.
Lincoln 14/1/28.
Immingham 3/2/37.
Mexborough 18/3/40.
Lincoln 22/12/46.

RENUMBERED:
5181 28/11/25.
1684 22/9/46.

CONDEMNED: 1/5/47.
Cut up at Gorton.

5182

Beyer, Peacock 4533.

To traffic 1/1904.

REPAIRS:
Gor. 21/7—27/8/09.**G.**
Gor. 26/10—21/12/12.**G.**
Gor. 2/1—1/5/15.**G.**
Gor. 7/6/19—20/3/20.**G.**
Ash ejector fitted.
Gor. 8/4—27/5/22.**G.**
Ross 'pops' fitted.
Gor. 15/3—12/7/24.**G.**
Gor. 20/2—30/6/26.**G.**
Gor. 13/8—8/10/27.**G.**
Gor. 26/1—16/3/29.**G.**
Gor. 22/11—31/12/30.**G.**
Gor. 11/3—15/4/33.**G.**
Superheated boiler fitted.
Gor. 28/10—18/11/33.**L.**
Gor. 23/3—13/4/35.**G.**
Gor. 16/1—6/2/37.**G.**
Gor. 6—20/5/39.**G.**
Gor. 14/11—13/12/41.**G.**
Gor. 26/6—24/7/43.**G.**
Gor. 18/5—29/6/46.**H.**
Gor. 25/10/47.**L.**
R.H. cylinder fractured.

BOILERS:
827.
829 *(ex5184)* 27/8/09.

Ramsbottom safety valves were used originally but on Diagram 17 boilers Ross 'pops' were standard. They could be either mounted directly on firebox - as in the previous photograph - or on what had first been prepared for the Ramsbottom safety valves. No.5183 changed to this saturated boiler in June 1933; it had been built early in 1923 for Q4 class.

Some of the original B5 design boilers acquired Ross 'pop' safety valves which had become standard in the early 1920's. Note that the smokebox ash ejector is on the left hand side as engine is not superheated.

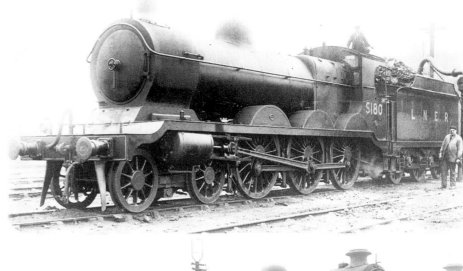

Superheated engines had the ash ejector on the right hand side with the steam supply pipe taken to the front end of the smokebox.

In August 1924, No.5184, the engine with the 5ft 0in. diameter boiler was again rebuilt, being fitted with 21in. diameter cylinders and piston valves. The same boiler was used but was then fitted with an anti-vacuum valve on the right hand end of the header. It only remained as shown to August 1927. Guide Bridge.

When they acquired a Diagram 17 superheated boiler, a Gresley anti-vacuum valve was fitted centrally behind the chimney.

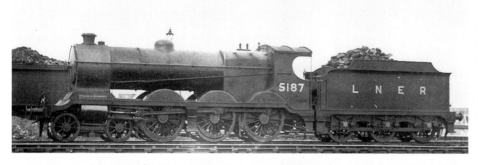

Even with superheating, and on Nos.6067, 6072, 5180, 5183, 5184, 5185 and 5187, which were rebuilt with 21in. cylinders and piston valves, front end lubrication was always sight feed from the cab. None was ever fitted with mechanical lubrication. Doncaster shed.

The whole class had wheel and handle fastening for the smokebox door and No.6070, scrapped in March 1939, remained so fitted. Note that although a saturated engine, the ash ejector steam pipe has been moved to the right hand side with front end entry.

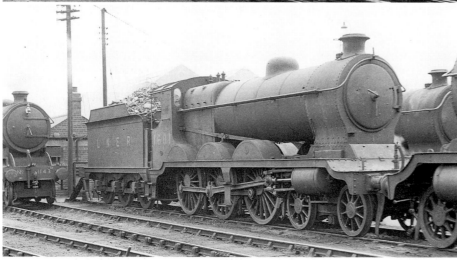

During the war most of the class had the wheel replaced by a second handle. Not all were so altered, No.1678 last repaired in January 1945, having a wheel at its November 1947 withdrawal (*see* page 75, bottom). Note that although the chimney is a 1934 design, it is taller than the standard 1ft 3in. for the class; compare with the illustration on page 71, second from bottom. Lincoln (GN) shed, May 1947.

5182 continued.
341 *(ex6069)* 21/12/12.
343 *(ex5183)* 1/5/15.
1844 *(new)* 20/3/20.
1777 *(ex5186)* 30/6/26.
1796 *(ex6069)* 31/12/30.
1901 *(exQ4 6142)* 15/4/33.
723 *(ex5185)* 6/2/37.
841 *(ex5185)* 20/5/39.
3721 *(exQ4 5153)* 24/7/43.

SHEDS:
Immingham *at* 1914.
Lincoln 14/1/28.
Sheffield 3/2/36.
Mexborough 31/5/43.
Lincoln 22/12/46.
Mexborough 14/7/47.

RENUMBERED:
5182 12/7/24.
1685 27/10/46.

CONDEMNED: 6/3/48.
Cut up at Dukinfield.

5183

Beyer, Peacock 4534.

To traffic 2/1904.

REPAIRS:
Gor. 21/9—9/11/07.**G.**
Gor. 4/8—4/11/11.**G.**
Gor. 12/12/14—23/1/15.**G.**
Gor. 23/6—4/8/17.**G.**
Gor. 14/9—1/12/19.**G.**
Gor. 30/10—25/12/20.**G.**
Gor. 20/1—16/6/23.**G.**
Gor. 31/1—4/4/25.**G.**
Gor. 1/10—26/11/27.**G.**
Gor. 18/5—22/6/29.**G.**
Gor. 7/3—11/4/31.**G.**
Gor. 6/5—3/6/33.**G.**
Gor. 22/6—13/7/35.**G.**
Superheated boiler fitted.
Gor. 9/5—20/6/36.**G.**
21in type 8K cylinders fitted.
Gor. 21/5—18/6/38.**G.**
Gor. 18/11—9/12/39.**G.**
Gor. 22/1—20/2/43.**G.**
Gor. 3—14/10/44.**G.**
Gor. 8/2—15/3/47.**G.**

BOILERS:
828.
338 *(ex6067)* 9/11/07.
343 *(ex6072)* 4/11/11.
825 *(ex5185)* 23/1/15.
342 *(ex6070)* 4/8/17.
1777 *(new)* 1/2/19.
468 *(new)* 16/6/23.
439 *(exQ4 5161)* 22/6/29.
418 *(exQ4 5068)* 3/6/33.

903 *(exQ4 6142)* 13/7/35.
875 *(exQ4 5057)* 18/6/38.
899 *(exB9 6106)* 9/12/39.
837 *(exB9 6111)* 20/2/43.
3733 *(Q4 5068)* 14/10/44.
3729 *(ex5185)* 15/3/47.

SHEDS:
Immingham 19/5/22.
Ardsley 5/1/24.
Gorton 15/4/24.
Lincoln 20/4/25.
Sheffield 20/6/36.
Trafford Park 6/10/46.
Mexborough 24/8/47.

RENUMBERED:
5183 4/4/25.
1686 31/3/46.

CONDEMNED: 12/6/50.
Into Gor. for cut up 17/6/50.

5184

Beyer, Peacock 4535.

To traffic 2/1904.

REPAIRS:
Gor. 6/2—6/3/09.**G.**
Gor. 11/11/10—14/1/11.**G.**
Gor. 13/5/16—20/1/17.**G.**
Gor. 16/9—9/6/23.**G.**
*8K superheated boiler & side
window cab fitted.*
Gor. 19—26/1/24.**L.**
Gor. 24/5—2/8/24.**G.**
21in type 8K cylinders fitted.
Gor. 18/7—3/10/25.**G.**
Gor. 6/8—10/12/27.**G.**
8A boiler & ordinary cab fitted.
Gor. 20/4—25/5/29.**G.**
Gor. 23/5—20/6/31.**G.**
Gor. 23/12/33—20/1/34.**G.**
Gor. 25/4—16/5/36.**G.**
Gor. 14—28/5/38.**G.**
Gor. 13/1—3/2/40.**G.**
Gor. 15—22/2/41.**L.**
After collision.
Gor. 16/4—8/5/43.**G.**
Gor. 18/5—29/6/46.**G.**
Gor. 4/7/47. *Not repaired.*

BOILERS:
829.
825 *(ex5180)* 6/3/09.
830 *(ex5181)* 14/1/11.
1288 *(ex6069)* 20/1/17.
1514 *(exO4 6194)* 9/6/23.
837 *(new)* 10/12/27.
910 *(exQ4 5164)* 20/6/31.
589 *(exQ4 6182)* 20/1/34.
640 *(new)* 16/5/36.
894 *(ex5186)* 28/5/38.

650 *(exB9 6114)* 3/2/40.
3727 *(exQ4 5163)* 8/5/43.
138 *(ex6068)* 29/6/46.

SHEDS:
Immingham 19/5/22.
Ardsley 5/1/24.
Gorton 16/4/24.
Immingham 8/10/25.
Woodford 6/8/26.
Immingham 30/5/29.
Lincoln 24/7/30.
Immingham 25/9/30.
Lincoln 6/7/37.
Immingham 3/9/37.
Doncaster 15/3/40.
Mexborough 18/3/40.

RENUMBERED:
5184 26/1/24.
1687 22/9/46.

CONDEMNED: 4/7/47.
Cut up at Gorton.

5185

Beyer, Peacock 4536.

To traffic 2/1904.

REPAIRS:
Gor. 4/1—21/3/08.**G.**
Gor. 25/3—27/5/11.**G.**
Gor. 26/9—7/11/14.**G.**
Gor. 9/8/19—27/3/20.**G.**
Gor. 15/4—10/6/22.**G.**
Ross 'pops' fitted.
Gor. 13/10—1/12/23.**G.**
Gor. 28/3—4/7/25.**G.**
Gor. 18/2—26/5/28.**G.**
*Superheated boiler & 21in type
8K cylinders fitted.*
Gor. 9/11—14/12/29.**G.**
Gor. 30/1—13/2/32.**G.**
Gor. 22/7—12/8/33.**G.**
Gor. 23/2—9/3/35.**G.**
Gor. 31/12/36—16/1/37.**G.**
Gor. 12—26/11/38.**G.**
Gor. 8/2—1/3/41.**G.**
Gor. 17—28/3/42.**G.**
After collision.
Gor. 22/1—12/2/44.**G.**
Gor. 1/2—8/3/47.**G.**
Gor. 31/10/49. *Not repaired.*

BOILERS:
830.
831 *(ex5186)* 21/3/08.
825 *(ex5184)* 27/5/11.
739 *(ex6071)* 7/11/14.
1891 *(new)* 27/3/20.
495 *(new)* 1/12/23.
848 *(new)* 26/5/28.
407 *(ex6068)* 13/2/32.

1912 *(exB9 6113)* 12/8/33.
723 *(exQ4 6077)* 9/3/35.
841 *(exB9 6108)* 16/1/37.
722 *(ex6069)* 26/11/38.
3728 *(new)* 1/3/41.
3729 *(ex5181)* 12/2/44.
3738 *(exB9 6111)* 8/3/47.

SHEDS:
Gorton.
Ardsley 5/1/24.
Immingham 24/4/24.
Lincoln 15/8/24.
Woodford 16/6/30.
Ardsley 24/7/30.
Lincoln 22/8/30.
Mexborough 18/3/40.
Bradford 17/6/47.
Mexborough 7/9/47.

RENUMBERED:
185c 1/12/23.
5185 4/7/25.
1688 26/5/46.

CONDEMNED: 31/10/49.
Cut up at Dukinfield.

5186

Beyer, Peacock 4537.

To traffic 2/1904.

REPAIRS:
Gor. 19/10—23/11/07.**G.**
Gor. 24/6—2/9/11.**G.**
Gor. 8/2—8/3/13.**G.**
Gor. 25/1—9/8/19.**G.**
Gor. 6/8—22/10/21.**G.**
Gor. 5/5—14/7/23.**G.**
Gor. 15/8—24/10/25.**G.**
Gor. 5/12/25—30/1/26.**L.**
Gor. 19/11/27—28/1/28.**G.**
Superheated boiler fitted.
Gor. 27/7—14/9/29.**G.**
Gor. 16/5—20/6/31.**G.**
Gor. 21/1—4/2/33.**G.**
Gor. 15—29/9/34.**G.**
Gor. 16—30/5/36.**G.**
Gor. 19/2—19/3/38.**G.**
Gor. 25/1—22/2/41.**G.**
Gor. 11—27/6/42.**L.**
Gor. 13/5—10/6/44.**G.**
Gor. 10/8—14/9/46.**G.**

BOILERS:
831.
339 *(ex6068)* 23/11/07.
831 *(ex5185)* 2/9/11.
829 *(ex5182)* 8/3/13.
1796 *(new)* 9/8/19.
1777 *(ex5183)* 14/7/23.
165 *(ex6071)* 24/10/25.
893 *(new)* 28/1/28.

The standard position for the upper lamp iron remained on top of the smokebox. Note Neilson maker's plate still surviving on the leading splasher. Trafford Park shed, April 1947.

5186 continued.
916 *(new)* 20/6/31.
901 *(exQ4 5092)* 4/2/33.
47 *(exQ4 5138)* 29/9/34.
894 *(exQ4 6073)* 30/5/36.
525 *(exQ4 6132)* 19/3/38.
3728 *(ex5185)* 10/6/44.
869 *(exQ4 6054)* 14/9/46.

SHEDS:
Mexborough 15/12/22.
Ardsley 5/1/24.
Gorton 7/1/24.
Immingham 4/3/24.
Woodford 7/8/26.
Sheffield 31/3/36.
Mexborough 31/5/43.
Lincoln 22/12/46.
Mexborough 14/7/47.

RENUMBERED:
5186 24/10/25.
1311 31/1/46.
1689 24/3/46.

CONDEMNED: 19/10/49.
*Into Gor. for cut up 22/10/49
but cut up at Dukinfield.*

5187

Beyer, Peacock 4538.

To traffic 3/1904.

REPAIRS:
Gor. 7/5—4/6/10.**G.**
Gor. 24/12/11—27/1/12.**G.**
Gor. 9/3—14/12/18.**G.**
Gor. 25/2—20/5/22.**G.**
Gor. 16/2—26/4/24.**G.**
Gor. 2/10—26/12/26.**G.**
Gor. 24/11/28—19/1/29.**G.**
Gor. 21/6—26/7/30.**G.**
Superheated boiler fitted.
Gor. 11/7—5/9/31.**G.**
Gor. 25/11—9/12/33.**G.**
Gor. 24/8—21/9/35.**G.**
Gor. 6/2—13/3/37.**G.**
21in type 8K cylinders fitted.
Gor. 8—29/10/38.**G.**
Gor. 29/6—20/7/40.**G.**
Gor. 25/3—11/4/42.**L.**
Gor. 12/6—3/7/43.**G.**
Gor. 28/12/43—15/1/44.**L.**
After collision.
Gor. 27/10—17/11/45.**G.**

BOILERS:
832
1335 *(new)* 4/6/10.
339 *(ex5186)* 27/1/12.
1772 *(new)* 14/12/18.
1891 *(ex5185)* 26/4/24.
1844 *(ex5182)* 26/12/26.
642 *(ex6068)* 26/7/30.
893 *(ex5186)* 5/9/31.
725 *(ex6072)* 9/12/33.
495 *(ex6072)* 21/9/35.
874 *(exQ4 5160)* 29/10/38.
148 *(ex6069)* 20/7/40.
333 *(ex6068)* 3/7/43.
911 *(exQ4 6076)* 17/11/45.

SHEDS:
Lincoln 28/7/22.
Immingham 30/6/36.
Mexborough 18/3/40.

RENUMBERED:
5187 26/4/24.
1312 27/1/46.
1690 23/3/46.

CONDEMNED: 20/4/48.
*Into Gor. for cut up 24/4/48 but
cut up at Dukinfield.*

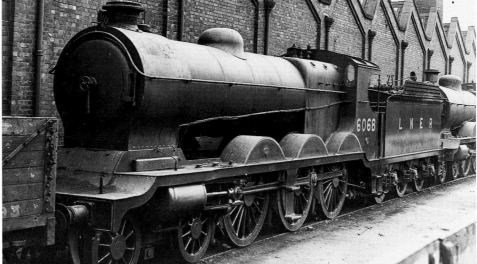

After rebuilding, some were fitted with a Group Standard lamp iron fixed to the front of the smokebox.

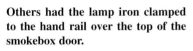

Others had the lamp iron clamped to the hand rail over the top of the smokebox door.

Three of the class, at least, had the top lamp iron duplicated by also having one fitted on the smokebox door. Those so noted were 5181, 5182 and 6069.

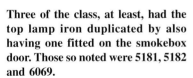

Most of the class retained GCR buffers with circular head but No.6067 acquired GS type during the war, as also did No.1688.

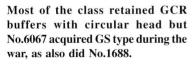

Amongst the fourteen in the class, four varieties of tender could be seen. No.6069 had a standard tender, built for J11 class No.6115, from Grouping to July 1940. This had solid coping with beading.

No.5184, from August 1924 to February 1940, had a tender from D9 class No.5106 which kept its open coal rails at least to January 1934. Nottingham (Victoria).

No.5183 had a similar tender to 6069 until June 1935. It then changed to this one with rails plated on the inside, which had been built for, and came from C4 class No.5267 on which the open rails had been retained at least to June 1933. Neepsend shed, June 1937.

No.1685 (ex 5182) from before Grouping through to withdrawal had a railed tender plated on the outside but without beading to the edge. This tender had been built for D9 class No.6019 and plated to GCR practice. Gorton works, March 1948.

First LNER paintings continued the black but with only single red lining, but they kept the large brass number plate except on No.184 on which a new cab was provided (*see* page 68, top). Only 185c and 1071c carried the area suffix, but 1068, 180, 181,183,186 got this numbering except for the suffix. No.1072 (ex paint shop 24th March 1923) is believed to have been the only one to have had L.&N.E.R. No.6070 was sent out on 19th April 1924 unpainted after a general repair so would simply have 6070 on a large brass number plate and had to wait to August 1926 for its LNER livery. No.5187 also went out unpainted on 26th April 1924 and did not get LNER until December 1926. Gorton shed.

(above) The remaining three, Nos.6067, 6069 and 5182 went to these numbers and LNER in October 1924, May 1925 and July 1924 respectively, and the others followed at their next shopping. No.6072 got the single red lining with that number in May 1925.

(right) Between March 1929 (No.5182) and June 1931 (No.6070) all had the number moved from the tender to the cab, but 6067, 6069, 6070, 5186 would have lost their red lining between September 1928 and February 1929 whilst the number was still on the tender. Immingham shed, June 1939.

77

From June 1931 to withdrawal, all fourteen were in unlined black but at least until 1939 the splasher beading on all except two (5184 and 6070) was not painted over, even if not always kept polished. Neepsend shed, October 1936.

No.184 had lost the beading to its splashers when ex works in June 1923 after getting the larger diameter boiler. The other to have the brass beading removed was 6070, probably in June 1931. All except No.6070, which was scrapped in March 1939, had their tender lettering reduced to NE during the war.

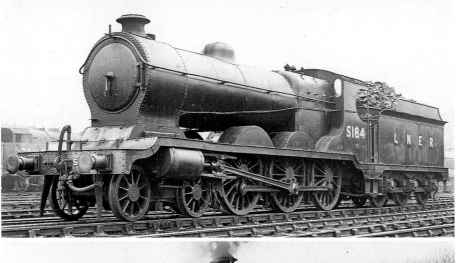

After the war Nos. 6068, 5182 and 5184 regained LNER before being renumbered, as also did Nos.1680, 1681, 1686 and 1688, shaded transfers being used for all except 1686.

Shaded transfers were used for Nos.1680 (August 1946), 1681 (December 1946) and 1688 (8th March 1947) when ex works after their last general repair and possibly for 1686 (15th March 1947). Trafford Park, 1947.

Nos.1678, 1682, 1683, 1684, 1685, 1687, 1689 and 1690 were put into their 1946 numbers at Mexborough shed, using 6in. stencils which were in Gill sans style with modified 6 and 9. Dukinfield works, after condemnation.

Nos.1679 and 1686 were renumbered at Darnall (Sheffield) shed and they used 12in. painted and unshaded numbers also in Gill sans style but with modified 6 and 9. Note cab number plate is still 5183. Darnall shed.

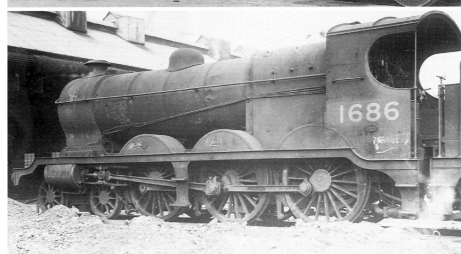

No.1689 at Gorton after its withdrawal on 19th October 1949. Note the heater connection at the front end. Although it had a general repair at Gorton in August/September 1946 either it had no attention to painting then or this photograph was taken in August 1946.

No.1690 being cut up at Dukinfield on 4th July 1948 after withdrawal on 20th April 1948. It was last shopped in November 1945 so retained only NE on its tender which was J11 type, coupled since July 1940 and still fitted with water pick-up gear.

Following another eight 2-8-0's, two more B6 (52 and 53) were built in 1921. They differed from the 1918 engine by having a double side window cab with a roof extension, and also had lower dome cover. Gorton shed.

After Grouping the first change was the removal of the header discharge valve and the combined circulating and blower valve, but a Gresley anti-vacuum valve was not provided until the late 1930's (*see* page 83, top). From 1926 a plant pot chimney replaced the GC type. Hull Dairycoates shed.

Only Ross 'pop' safety valves were used, but some of the O5 boilers which interchanged with those on B6 class had short 'pops' mounted on a base plate as shown here. Note the removal of the footsteps midway on the frame. 5053 also lost them, but 5416 did not. York, June 1932.

CLASS B 6

5416

Gorton.

To traffic 7/1918.

REPAIRS:
Gor. 25/9—30/10/20.**G.**
Gor. 30/9—9/12/22.**G.**
Gor. 31/1—21/3/25.**G.**
Gor. 5/2—9/4/27.**G.**
Gor. 16/2—23/3/29.**G.**
Gor. 7/6—12/7/30.**G.**
Gor. 24/1—28/3/31.**L.**
Gor. 13/2—5/3/32.**L.**
Gor. 8—29/4/33.**G.**
Gor. 18/5—6/7/35.**G.**
Intensifore removed.
Gor. 20/3—3/4/37.**G.**
Gor. 11—25/2/39.**G.**
Gor. 5/4—3/5/41.**G.**
Gor. 17/2—13/3/43.**G.**
Gor. 10—31/3/45.**G.**

BOILERS:
1734.
1725 *(exO5 5414)* 9/4/27.
 873 *(exO5 5014)* 29/4/33.
1726 *(exO5 5015)* 6/7/35.
1792 *(exO5 5415)* 3/4/37.
1789 *(ex5053)* 25/2/39.
3700 *(new)* 3/5/41.
 873 *(exO5 5422)* 13/3/43.
1726 *(exO5 5420)* 31/3/45.

SHEDS:
Gorton 14/7/22.
Sheffield 5/9/25.
Gorton 23/4/27.

Sheffield 7/5/27.
Ardsley 17/2/28.
Copley Hill 30/4/28.
Ardsley 1/10/28.
Bradford 15/6/29.
Sheffield 1/6/34.
Ardsley 28/7/46.

RENUMBERED:
5416 21/3/25.
1346 15/9/46.

CONDEMNED: 28/11/47.
Cut up at Dukinfield.

5052

Gorton.

To traffic 3/1921.

REPAIRS:
Gor. 24/2—24/4/23.**G.**
Gor. 11—25/8/23.**L.**
Gor. 28/11/25—6/2/26.**G.**
Gor. 12/11/27—7/1/28.**G.**
Gor. 5/7—2/8/30.**G.**
Gor. 24/6—15/7/33.**G.**
Gor. 13—27/7/35.**G.**
Intensifore removed.
Gor. 30/1—20/2/37.**G.**
New R.H. cylinder fitted.
Gor. 27/5—17/6/39.**G.**
Gor. 4—23/8/41.**G.**
Gor. 18/1—12/2/44.**G.**
Gor. 29/6—3/8/46.**G.**
Gor. 24/5—14/6/47.**L.**
Gor. 31/12/47. *Not repaired.*

BOILERS:
 58.
 64 *(ex5053)* 2/8/30.
 873 *(ex5416)* 27/7/35.
 2 *(ex5053)* 20/2/37.
 64 *(exO5 5010)* 23/8/41.
3699 *(ex5053)* 12/2/44.
3700 *(ex5053)* 3/8/46.

SHEDS:
Gorton 14/7/22.
Sheffield 10/2/26.
Ardsley 7/2/28.
Bradford 13/5/30.
Ardsley 10/9/30.
Bradford 29/12/30.
Ardsley 14/4/31.
Sheffield 15/5/34.
Ardsley 4/8/46.

RENUMBERED:
 52c 25/8/23.
5052 6/2/26.
1347 12/5/46.

CONDEMNED: 31/12/47.
Cut up at Dukinfield.

5053

Gorton.

To traffic 4/1921.

REPAIRS:
Gor. 9/6—18/8/23.**G.**
Gor. 26/6—2/10/26.**G.**
Gor. 29/9—12/1/29.**G.**
Gor. 17/10—21/11/31.**G.**

Gor. 15/9—6/10/34.**G.**
Intensifore removed & a new R.H. cylinder fitted.
Gor. 20/6—4/7/36.**G.**
Gor. 19/6—3/7/37.**L.**
Gor. 21—28/1/39.**G.**
Gor. 22/2—22/3/41.**G.**
Gor. 11—28/8/43.**G.**
Gor. 15/1—9/2/46.**G.**
Gor. 31/12/47. *Not repaired.*

BOILERS:
 64.
 2 *(exO5 5017)* 12/1/29.
1789 *(exO5 5418)* 4/7/36.
 1 *(exO5 5010)* 28/1/39.
3699 *(new)* 22/3/41.
3700 *(ex5416)* 28/8/43.
 64 *(ex5052)* 9/2/46.

SHEDS:
Gorton 14/7/22.
Sheffield 2/2/27.
Ardsley 17/2/28.
Copley Hill 26/3/28.
Ardsley 30/4/28.
Bradford 1/2/30.
Sheffield 26/6/34.
Ardsley 28/7/46.

RENUMBERED:
 53c 18/8/23.
5053 2/10/26.
1348 18/8/46.

CONDEMNED: 31/12/47.
Cut up at Gorton.

The original tender with No.5416 had Iracier axleboxes but in February 1932 this was replaced by a standard tender from D11 class No.5509. Note the heater connection fitted at the front end. Intensifore was replaced by Wakefield mechanical lubrication in July 1935.

(left) From 1935 the plant pot chimney was replaced by one more like the original on all three engines. 5052 had the Intensifore changed to Wakefield lubricator in July 1935 and 5053 had been changed similarly in October 1934. No attempt was made to bring this class within the composite 13ft 0in. load gauge. Retford, May 1938.

(above) Original livery was goods black with red and white lining but without GCR crest or monogram. This painting was retained on the engine when ex paint shop on 27th January 1923 but the tender was changed from its Great Central and crest to 6in. L.& N.E.R. and number in 12in. shaded figures, the engine retaining its large brass number plate.

(left) At the end of August 1923, Nos.52 and 53 changed to single red lining with LNER and area suffix C to their number on the tender. They became 5416 on 21st March 1925, 5052 on 6th February 1926 and 5053 on 2nd October 1926. Note difference in shape of buffer heads between this one and 5416 in the next illustration, and compare with the view on page 81 and 5052 at the top of this page. 5053 had buffers like 5052 when new.

From March 1929 (5416), all had the number moved from the tender to cab, 5052 in August 1930 and 5053 in November 1931. The latter had lost its red lining in January 1929 whilst the number was still on the tender (*see* page 80, centre), and the other two when they got their numbers on the cab. Nottingham (Victoria).

(*centre*) No.5416 was last shopped in March 1945 and so retained only NE on its tender. When renumbered 1346 at Ardsley shed on Sunday 15th September 1946 it got 12in. painted and unshaded figures. Note that it retained the wheel and handle for the smokebox door fastening, and that the dome cover got a flat top. Ardsley shed.

(*below*) No.5053 regained LNER when ex works on 9th February 1946 without any alterations at the front end. On 18th August 1946 it was renumbered 1348 at Ardsley shed using 12in. painted and unshaded numbers. No.5052 became 1347 on 12th May 1946 but had a general repair from which it was ex works on 3rd August 1946. LNER was restored to the tender and this, and cab number were in shaded block transfers. Unlike the other two engines the smokebox door wheel was replaced by a second handle. The top lamp iron was moved from the handrail on to the door and GS buffer stocks were fitted though using GC style oval heads. Dukinfield works.

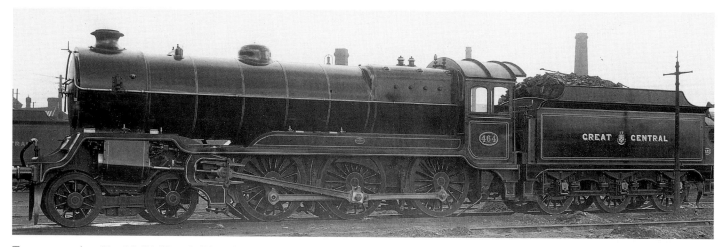

Ten more engines Nos.36, 37, 38 and 458 to 464, were built between September and November 1921 by Vulcan Foundry. They were the same as the first three except for separate control to the blower and omission of steam circulating valve. Gorton shed.

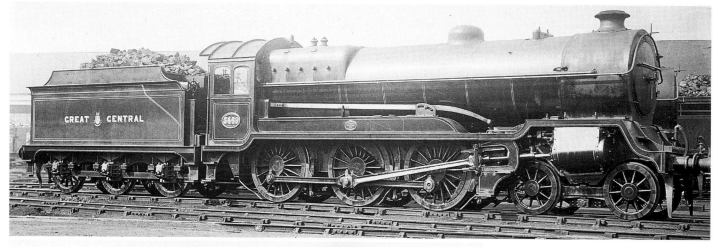

(above) Ten further engines, Nos.465 to 474, were built from August 1921 to August 1922 by Gorton. These were the same as the Vulcan engines with separate blower control but had also a smokebox ash ejector with steam supply pipe entering at the rear. This engine's tender was repainted in January 1923 for the Director's Group Livery selection at York on 31st January 1923. Gorton shed.

(left) Another five engines, Nos.31 to 35, were built during July and August 1922 to same design, by Beyer, Peacock & Co. They had the combined steam circulating valve and blower control.

Gorton built six more engines, Nos. 475 to 479 and 5481, during the period August to December 1923. They were of similar design but the boiler mountings and cab heights were cut to conform to the 13ft 0in. composite load gauge. Note muffled type Ross 'pop' safety valves. These cut-down engines were Part 2. The steam supply to the ash ejector was now moved to enter the front end of the smokebox (see next illustration).

CLASS B 7

5072

Gorton.

To traffic 5/1921.

REPAIRS:
Gor. 11/8—3/11/23.**G**.
Gor. 1/8—7/11/25.**G**.
Gor. 9/4—18/6/27.**G**.
Gor. 16/3—11/5/29.**G**.
Gor. 7/3—11/4/31.**G**.
Gor. 11/3—1/4/33.**G**.
Gor. 29/9—13/10/34.**G**.
Gor. 25/4—16/5/36.**G**.
Gor. 19/6—17/7/37.**G**.
Gor. 26/11—17/12/38.**G**.
Gor. 24/8—28/9/40.**G**.
Gor. 27/2—20/3/43.**G**.
Gor. 16/6—4/8/45.**G**.
Gor. 28/9—5/10/46.**L**.
Gor. 18—25/1/47.**L**.
After collision.

BOILERS:
65.
1921 *(ex5036)* 18/6/27.
80 *(exB3 6168)* 11/4/31.
1931 *(ex5464)* 1/4/33.
1932 *(ex5481)* 13/10/34.
267 *(ex5458)* 16/5/36.
791 *(ex5078)* 17/7/37.
3002 *(ex5034)* 17/12/38.
784 *(ex5031)* 28/9/40.
86 *(ex5460)* 20/3/43.

SHEDS:
Gorton 25/5/21.
Immingham 26/6/27.
Gorton 9/5/29.
Woodford 5/3/37.
Gorton 30/10/43.
Darnall 20/10/46.

RENUMBERED:
72c 3/11/23.
5072 7/11/25.
1360 3/11/46.

CONDEMNED: 10/9/48.
*Into Gor. for cut up 11/9/48 but
sent via Dukinfield to
Darlington and cut up 11/48.*

5073

Gorton.

To traffic 6/1921.

REPAIRS:
Gor. 1/9—17/11/23.**G**.
Gor. 1/8—14/11/25.**G**.
Gor. 9/4—4/6/27.**G**.
Gor. 9/3—20/4/29.**G**.
Gor. 2/5—6/6/31.**G**.
Gor. 13/5—17/6/33.**G**.
Gor. 17/2—17/3/34.**L**.
Gor. 17/11—8/12/34.**G**.
Gor. 11/7—8/8/36.**G**.
Gor. 26/2—19/3/38.**G**.
Gor. 24/2—30/3/40.**G**.
Gor. 12/1—13/2/43.**G**.
Gor. 4—25/11/44.**G**.
Gor. 3/5—14/6/47.**G**.

BOILERS:
69.
160 *(ex5467)* 4/6/27.
69 *(ex5478)* 17/6/33.
77 *(exB8 5004)* 8/12/34.
559 *(ex5482)* 8/8/36.
3021 *(new)* 19/3/38.
3011 *(exB8 5442)* 30/3/40.
3037 *(new)* 13/2/43.
3022 *(ex5465)* 25/11/44.
3037 *(ex1380)* 14/6/47.

SHEDS:
Gorton 25/6/21.
Immingham 23/6/31.
Gorton 9/8/31.
Woodford 22/1/37.
Gorton 24/10/43.
Darnall 1/7/45.

RENUMBERED:
73c 17/11/23.
5073 14/11/25.
1361 21/8/46.

CONDEMNED: 4/3/49.
Cut up at Dukinfield.

5078

Gorton.

To traffic 7/1921.

REPAIRS:
Gor. 15/12/23—1/3/24.**G**.
Gor. 8/5—4/9/26.**G**.
Gor. 9/6—29/9/28.**G**.
Gor. 5/7—16/8/30.**G**.
Gor. 28/5—18/6/32.**G**.
Gor. 9/6—7/7/34.**G**.
Gor. 25/1—15/2/36.**G**.
Gor. 12/6—3/7/37.**G**.
Gor. 14/1—4/2/39.**G**.
Gor. 2—23/11/40.**G**.
Gor. 19/5—12/6/43.**G**.
Gor. 13/1—17/2/45.**G**.
Gor. 26/4—24/5/47.**G**.

BOILERS:
73.
1927 *(ex5461)* 4/9/26.
1848 *(exB2 5423)* 29/9/28.
503 *(ex5480)* 18/6/32.
791 *(ex5464)* 15/2/36.
763 *(ex5476)* 3/7/37.
1922 *(exB2 5423)* 4/2/39.
583 *(ex5464)* 23/11/40.
3017 *(exB2 5423)* 12/6/43.
791 *(ex5038)* 17/2/45.
3019 *(exB8 1357)* 24/5/47.

SHEDS:
Gorton 30/7/21.
Immingham 27/8/32.
Gorton 20/10/32.
Woodford 20/2/36.
Gorton 30/10/43.
Darnall 1/7/45.

RENUMBERED:
5078 1/3/24.
1362 15/9/46.

CONDEMNED: 20/4/49.
*Into Gor. for cut up 23/4/49 but
cut up at Dukinfield.*

5036

Vulcan 3478.

To traffic 9/1921.

REPAIRS:
Gor. 8/3—17/5/24.**G**.
Gor. 14/8—30/10/26.**G**.
Gor. 23/6—27/10/28.**G**.
Gor. 31/5—19/7/30.**G**.
Gor. 6—27/8/32.**G**.
Gor. 26/5—23/6/34.**G**.

Gor. 9—30/11/35.**G**.
Gor. 27/3—24/4/37.**G**.
Gor. 1/4—6/5/39.**G**.
Gor. 13/4—25/5/40.**G**.
Four new cylinders fitted.
Gor. 13/4—9/5/42.**G**.
Gor. 30/12/43—19/2/44.**G**.
Gor. 3—24/11/45.**G**.
Gor. 11/1/47.**L**.
Gor. 8—22/3/47.**L**.
After collision.
Gor. 21/6/47.**L**.
Gor. 12/6/48. *Not repaired.*

BOILERS:
1921.
73 *(ex5078)* 30/10/26.
263 *(ex5468)* 27/10/28.
354 *(exB8 5004)* 27/8/32.
1934 *(exB2 5425)* 23/6/34.
3005 *(ex5476)* 30/11/35.
1849 *(ex5472)* 24/4/37.
3006 *(ex5462)* 6/5/39.
3021 *(ex5073)* 25/5/40.
244 *(ex5482)* 9/5/42.
3011 *(exB8 5444)* 24/11/45.

SHEDS:
Neasden 4/11/21.
Immingham 3/2/22.
Woodford 12/1/23.
Gorton 24/5/24.
Annesley 10/6/25.
Colwick 4/3/26.
Gorton 1/4/26.
Neasden 5/12/39.
Woodford 24/12/39.
Gorton 30/10/43.
Darnall 25/6/45.

RENUMBERED:
5036 17/5/24.
1363 4/10/46.

CONDEMNED: 12/6/48.
Cut up at Dukinfield.

5037

Vulcan 3479.

To traffic 10/1921.

REPAIRS:
Gor. 6/10—1/12/23.**G**.
Gor. 11/7—10/10/25.**G**.
Gor. 16/4—11/6/27.**G**.

WORKS CODES:- Cw - Cowlairs. Dar- Darlington. Don - Doncaster. Ghd - Gateshead. Gor - Gorton. Inv - Inverurie. Str - Stratford.
REPAIR CODES:- **C/H** - Casual Heavy. **C/L** - Casual Light. **G** - General. **H**- Heavy. **H/I** - Heavy Intermediate. **L** - Light. **L/I** - Light Intermediate. **N/C** - Non-Classified.

85

(*above*) **Four final engines, Nos.480, 5482, 5483 and 5484, were built between 24th November 1923 and 1st March 1924 by Gorton. They had a larger steam chest to accommodate valves having more widely spaced heads, steam passages were straighter and the cylinder casings were vertical instead of inclined. Each of the four cylinders had a relief valve with a cover on the apron plate. Nottingham (Victoria).**

(*centre*) **As No.5468 (1376 later) in March 1936, four new cylinders were fitted to a Part 1 engine and these were of the later design but the cylinder relief valves were subsequently removed. Nos.5033, 5036, 5038, 5461, 5462, 5464 to 5469, 5471 and 5472 were so fitted between March 1936 and December 1947. Sheffield, January 1947.**

All thirty-eight engines were built with frames ending with a concave curve at the front (*see* previous views). However, during the war, trouble was experienced with buckling and cracking of the frames in the vicinity of the cylinders. To strengthen the frames, at least fifteen of the class had a curved addition welded to the front end of the frames.

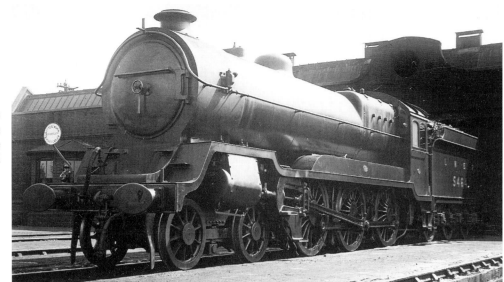

The whole class were fitted with Robinson top feed apparatus to the boiler, with casing between the chimney and dome, and most retained it until after 1930. Neasden shed.

There were however some early removals, No.5467 losing it before this engine was fitted with a built-up chimney which it got either in June 1926 or in December 1927.

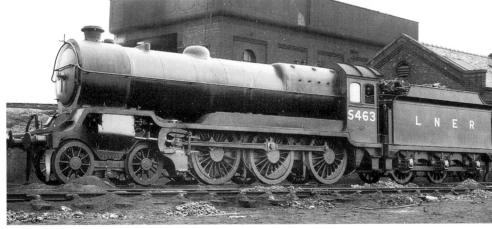

On most of the class top feed could be seen in conjunction with built-up chimney and Gresley anti-vacuum valve.

Top feed survived at least to August 1936 on No.5460, which appears to have been the last to be recorded so fitted. It could be that the top feed lasted to January 1938 as this boiler on 5460 was 5473's original and was used on 5460 from September 1936 to January 1938. Certainly by September 1939 all top feed had been removed, but patched boiler cladding still provided evidence of its fitting. Neasden shed.

5037 continued.
Gor. 30/3—11/5/29.**G.**
Gor. 28/2—28/3/31.**G.**
Gor. 1—22/4/33.**G.**
Gor. 15/12/34—12/1/35.**G.**
Gor. 14/12/35—11/1/36.**G.**
New inside cylinders fitted.
Gor. 22/1—19/2/38.**G.**
Gor. 23/12/39—13/1/40.**G.**
Gor. 29/3—26/4/41.**L.**
After collision.
Gor. 9/2—7/3/42.**G.**
Gor. 27/1—26/2/44.**G.**
Gor. 22/6—3/8/46.**G.**
Gor. 12/6/48. *Not repaired.*

BOILERS:
1922.
1923 *(ex5038)* 11/6/27.
 397 *(exB3 6166)* 28/3/31.
 80 *(ex5072)* 22/4/33.
 69 *(ex5073)* 12/1/35.
 263 *(exB8 5004)* 11/1/36.
 526 *(ex5482)* 19/2/38.
 6 *(ex5468)* 13/1/40.
 631 *(ex5466)* 7/3/42.
3041 *(ex5481)* 26/2/44.
3039 *(ex5464)* 3/8/46.

SHEDS:
Neasden 4/11/21.
Immingham 3/2/22.
Woodford 26/1/23.
Annesley 19/7/24.
Woodford 22/11/24.
Colwick 28/10/25.
Gorton 7/4/26.
Brunswick 11/8/40.
Gorton 20/9/40.
Annesley 3/5/43.
Gorton 30/10/43.
Darnall 25/6/45.
Gorton 16/4/47.

RENUMBERED:
 37c 1/12/23.
5037 10/10/25.
1364 10/10/46.

CONDEMNED: 12/6/48.
Cut up at Gorton.

5038

Vulcan 3480.

To traffic 10/1921.

REPAIRS:
Gor. 24/11/23—22/3/24.**G.**
Gor. 13/2—24/4/26.**G.**
Gor. 30/7—24/9/27.**G.**
Gor. 9/2—30/3/29.**G.**
Gor. 27/9—8/11/30.**G.**

Gor. 6/2—5/3/32.**G.**
Gor. 4/11—9/12/33.**G.**
Gor. 31/8—12/10/35.**G.**
New inside cylinders fitted.
Gor. 30/1—27/2/37.**G.**
Gor. 23/7—20/8/38.**G.**
Gor. 6—27/7/40.**G.**
Gor. 16/11—28/12/40.**H.**
Gor. 5/11—12/12/42.**G.**
Gor. 16/12/44—20/1/45.**G.**
Gor. 22/3—26/4/47.**G.**

BOILERS:
1923.
 610 *(new)* 24/4/26.
 424 *(exB2 5426)* 30/3/29.
 554 *(ex5471)* 5/3/32.
 345 *(ex5471)* 9/12/33.
 554 *(ex5475)* 12/10/35.
 424 *(ex5483)* 27/2/37.
 576 *(exB2 5427)* 20/8/38.
3020 *(ex5466)* 27/7/40.
 791 *(ex5034)* 12/12/42.
3003 *(ex5462)* 20/1/45.
 81 *(ex1382)* 26/4/47.

SHEDS:
Neasden 14/10/21.
Gorton 3/2/22.
Immingham 28/7/22.
Woodford 28/1/23.
Gorton 30/10/43.
Darnall 25/6/45.

RENUMBERED:
5038 22/3/24.
1365 31/7/46.
61702 7/5/49.

CONDEMNED: 13/6/49.
Cut up at Dukinfield.

5458

Vulcan 3481.

To traffic 10/1921.

REPAIRS:
Gor. 18/8—3/11/23.**G.**
Gor. 20/9—22/11/24.**G.**
Gor. 22—29/8/25.**L.**
Gor. 31/10/25—16/1/26.**G.**
Gor. 3/9—29/10/27.**G.**
Gor. 11—25/8/28.**L.**
Re-tubing.
Gor. 21/9—2/11/29.**G.**
Gor. 23/1—20/2/32.**G.**
Gor. 14/1—4/2/33.**G.**
Gor. 30/6—28/7/34.**G.**
Gor. 29/2—21/3/36.**G.**
Gor. 14/5—18/6/38.**G.**
Gor. 8—29/6/40.**G.**
Gor. 4—25/1/41.**L.**

After collision.
Gor. 1/10—28/11/42.**G.**
Gor. 11/11—2/12/44.**G.**
Gor. 18/1—15/2/47.**G.**

BOILERS:
1924.
 556 *(new)* 22/11/24.
1924 *(ex5459)* 20/2/32.
 267 *(exB3 6164)* 4/2/33.
 354 *(ex5035)* 21/3/36.
 559 *(ex5073)* 18/6/38.
 354 *(exB8 5446)* 29/6/40.
 81 *(exB8 5443)* 28/11/42.
3009 *(exB8 5442)* 2/12/44.
3044 *(ex1370)* 15/2/47.

SHEDS:
Neasden 18/11/21.
Gorton 21/11/24.
Neasden 3/9/25.
Gorton 16/1/26.
Colwick 9/2/26.
Gorton 1/4/26.
Woodford 2/11/42.
Annesley 24/5/43.
Woodford 21/6/43.
Annesley 5/7/43.
Gorton 30/10/43.

RENUMBERED:
 458c 3/11/23.
5458 22/11/24.
1366 20/7/46

CONDEMNED: 31/12/48.
Cut up at Gorton.

5459

Vulcan 3482.

To traffic 10/1921.

REPAIRS:
Gor. 6/10/23—19/1/24.**G.**
Gor. 7/11/25—13/2/26.**G.**
Gor. 10/12/27—25/2/28.**G.**
Gor. 1/3—12/4/30.**G.**
Gor. 21/11—31/12/31.**G.**
Gor. 30/12/33—31/1/34.**G.**
Gor. 14/9—5/10/35.**G.**
Gor. 7/8—4/9/37.**G.**
Gor. 29/7—26/8/39.**G.**
Gor. 12/2—14/3/42.**G.**
Gor. 22/5—19/6/43.**G.**
Gor. 17/3—21/4/45.**G.**
Gor. 14/6—9/8/47.**G.**

BOILERS:
1925.
1924 *(exB3 6167)* 25/2/28.
1929 *(ex5472)* 31/12/31.
1849 *(ex5480)* 20/1/34.

571 *(exB3 6166)* 5/10/35.
1846 *(ex5032)* 4/9/37.
3025 *(new)* 26/8/39.
3032 *(exB2 5426)* 19/6/43.
3017 *(ex5078)* 21/4/45.
3007 *(exB8 1359)* 9/8/47.

SHEDS:
Neasden 25/11/21.
Immingham 20/2/26.
Neasden 18/7/29.
Woodford 27/9/41.
Gorton 30/10/43.

RENUMBERED:
 459c 19/1/24.
5459 13/2/26.
1367 27/7/46.
61703 7/5/49.

CONDEMNED: 5/9/49.
Cut up at Dukinfield.

5460

Vulcan 3483.

To traffic 10/1921.

REPAIRS:
Gor. 9/2—19/4/24.**G.**
Gor. 19/12/25—6/3/26.**G.**
Gor. 14/4—26/5/28.**G.**
Gor. 21/12/29—1/2/30.**G.**
Gor. 19/9—24/10/31.**G.**
Gor. 22/7—12/8/33.**G.**
Gor. 5—26/1/35.**G.**
Gor. 22/8—26/9/36.**G.**
Gor. 15/1—5/2/38.**G.**
Gor. 3—17/9/38.**L.**
Gor. 27/1—24/2/40.**G.**
Gor. 13/4—18/5/40.**L.**
After collision.
Gor. 4/12/42—2/1/43.**G.**
Gor. 3/12/43—1/1/44.**G.**
Gor. 29/6—3/8/46.**G.**

BOILERS:
1926.
1925 *(ex5459)* 26/5/28.
 65 *(ex5463)* 24/10/31.
1923 *(ex5032)* 12/8/33.
 534 *(ex5473)* 26/1/35.
 295 *(exB8 5279)* 26/9/36.
3010 *(ex5031)* 5/2/38.
 86 *(ex5471)* 24/2/40.
 51 *(ex5481)* 2/1/43.
3027 *(ex5478)* 1/1/44.
3043 *(exB8 5279)* 3/8/46.

SHEDS:
Neasden 2/12/21.
Woodford 8/10/35.
Annesley 5/9/43.

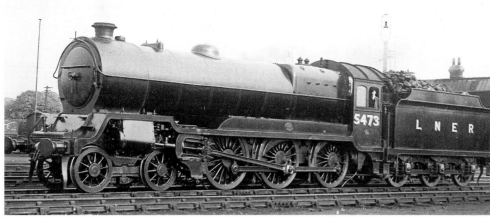

The whole class originally had Robinson's patent sight feed lubricator known as Intensifore. The lubrication by this system had the same arrangement on both sides of the engine.

The Intensifore lubrication was removed from June 1932 onwards and the process was completed when No.5034 lost it on 5th September 1936. It was taken off 5072 on 13th October 1934, being replaced by the Wakefield mechanical.

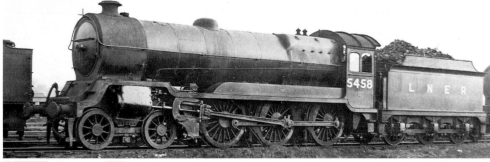

After some variations, the standard lubrication for the class settled down as Detroit or Eureka sight feed in the cab for cylinders and valves, with a Wakefield mechanical serving the coupled axleboxes. Neasden shed.

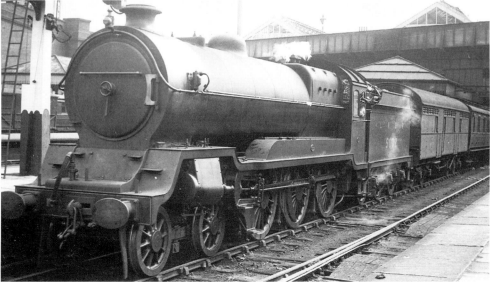

For the superheater element protection, the class started with the combined steam circulation valve with blower control, supplemented by a header discharge valve. Both were in evidence on the left-hand side of the smokebox. Nottingham (Victoria).

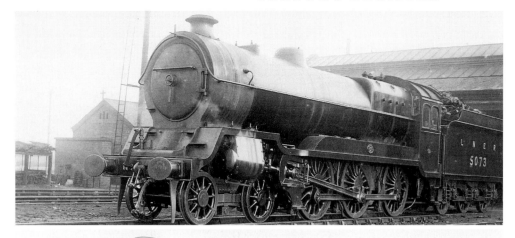

In the mid-1920's changes began, and No.5073 has lost the header discharge valve, but retains the earlier method of steam circulation combined with blower control.

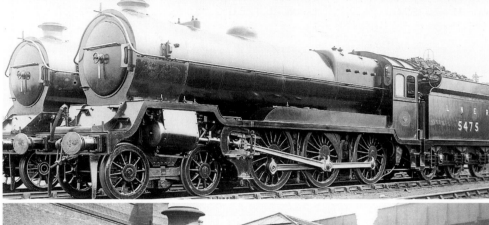

The Part 2 engines all had header discharge valve fitted and their smokeboxes had been prepared for the steam circulation connection to the cab but none of these ten had that method fitted.

After Grouping some of the class did not have any visible equipment for protection of the superheater elements from burning when the regulator was closed. *See* page 87, second illustration from top showing another example. Nottingham (Victoria).

By the middle 1920's the superiority and simplicity of the Gresley anti-vacuum valve was recognised and it quickly became standard on B7 class in its normal central position. Nottingham (Victoria).

5460 continued.
Gorton 30/10/43.

RENUMBERED:
5460 19/4/24.
1368 3/8/46

CONDEMNED: 6/10/48.
Into Gor. for cut up 9/10/48 but cut up at Dukinfield.

5461

Vulcan 3484.

To traffic 11/1921.

REPAIRS:
Gor. 19/4—5/7/24.**G.**
Gor. 3/4—10/7/26.**G.**
Gor. 24/3—19/5/28.**G.**
Gor. 14/12/29—8/2/30.**G.**
Gor. 11/7—8/8/31.**G.**
Gor. 5/8—2/9/33.**G.**
Gor. 20/4—25/5/35.**G.**
Gor. 14/11—5/12/36.**G.**
Gor. 28/5—25/6/38.**G.**
Gor. 4—25/11/39.**G.**
Gor. 9/6—4/7/42.**G.**
Gor. 24/3—6/5/44.**G.**
Gor. 16/1—23/2/46.**G.**
Gor. 24/8—21/9/46.**G.**

BOILERS:
1927.
1845 *(exB3 6168)* 10/7/26.
1698 *(ex5462)* 8/8/31.
　65 *(ex5460)* 2/9/33.
　51 *(exB3 6164)* 25/5/35.
631 *(ex5465)* 5/12/36.
3015 *(ex5463)* 25/6/38.
263 *(ex5470)* 25/11/39.
3005 *(ex5033)* 4/7/42.
3014 *(ex5033)* 6/5/44.
　51 *(ex5035)* 23/2/46.

SHEDS:
Neasden 9/12/21.
Doncaster 2/5/34.
Neasden 12/9/34.
Woodford 10/10/35.
Gorton 10/10/43.
Darnall 20/10/46.
Gorton 16/4/47.

RENUMBERED:
5461 5/7/24.
1369 22/11/46.

CONDEMNED: 21/8/48.
Cut up at Dukinfield.

5462

Vulcan 3485.

To traffic 11/1921.

REPAIRS:
Gor. 1/12/23—15/3/24.**G.**
Gor. 27/2—29/5/26.**G.**
Gor. 18/2—7/4/28.**G.**
Gor. 26/10—30/11/29.**G.**
Gor. 13/6—11/7/31.**G.**
Gor. 15/7—5/8/33.**G.**
Gor. 27/7—17/8/35.**G.**
Gor. 13/2—27/3/37.**G.**
New cylinders fitted.
Gor. 11—25/3/39.**G.**
Gor. 21/12/40—25/1/41.**G.**
Gor. 20/7—15/8/42.**G.**
Gor. 28/10—25/11/44.**G.**
Gor. 30/11/46—4/1/47.**G.**
Gor. 13/12/47—17/1/48.**H.**
After collision.
Gor. 19/11/48. *Not repaired.*

BOILERS:
1928.
1698 *(exB2 5425)* 7/4/28.
　539 *(new)* 11/7/31.
　160 *(ex5073)* 5/8/33.
3006 *(new)* 17/8/35.
　267 *(ex5032)* 25/3/39.
3016 *(ex5469)* 25/1/41.
3003 *(exB3 6165)* 15/8/42.
3044 *(new)* 25/11/44.
　526 *(ex1393)* 4/1/47.
3017 *(ex1367)* 17/1/48.

SHEDS:
Neasden 9/12/21.
Woodford 19/5/22.
Gorton 5/6/26.
Neasden 25/1/27.
Woodford 23/8/28.
Neasden 14/9/28.
Woodford 14/3/29.
Neasden 11/10/35.
Sheffield 14/4/38.
Annesley 3/5/43.
Gorton 24/10/43.

RENUMBERED:
　5462 15/3/24.
　1370 2/11/46.
ᴇ**1370** 17/1/48.

CONDEMNED: 19/11/48.
Cut up at Dukinfield.

5463

Vulcan 3486.

To traffic 11/1921.

REPAIRS:
Gor. 22/12/23—15/3/24.**G.**
Gor. 14/11/25—20/2/26.**G.**
Gor. 26/11/27—28/1/28.**G.**
Gor. 29/6—27/7/29.**G.**
Gor. 30/5—4/7/31.**G.**
Gor. 12/8—16/9/33.**G.**
Gor. 18/5—8/6/35.**G.**
Gor. 19/12/36—16/1/37.**G.**
Gor. 14/5—4/6/38.**G.**
Gor. 6—27/1/40.**G.**
Gor. 16/6—25/7/42.**G.**
Gor. 30/5—24/6/44.**G.**
Gor. 27/7—17/8/46.**G.**

BOILERS:
1929.
　65 *(ex5072)* 28/1/28.
1847 *(ex5467)* 4/7/31.
　539 *(ex5462)* 16/9/33.
3004 *(new)* 8/6/35.
3015 *(new)* 16/1/37.
　300 *(exB3 6167)* 4/6/38.
3001 *(exB3 6169)* 27/1/40.
　8 *(ex5483)* 25/7/42.
　773 *(exB8 5004)* 24/6/44.
3024 *(ex5482)* 17/8/46.

SHEDS:
Neasden 9/12/21.
Woodford 12/1/23.
Annesley 19/7/24.
Neasden 15/11/24.
Woodford 17/11/24.
Gorton 30/10/43.

RENUMBERED:
　5463 15/3/24.
　1371 26/11/46.

CONDEMNED: 22/1/49.
Cut up at Dukinfield.

5464

Vulcan 3487.

To traffic 11/1921.

REPAIRS:
Gor. 9/2—26/4/24.**G.**
Gor. 2/8—6/9/24.**L.**
After collision.
Gor. 23/1—3/4/26.**G.**
Gor. 28/4—28/7/28.**G.**

Gor. 18/10—22/11/30.**G.**
Gor. 18/2—4/3/33.**G.**
Gor. 13—27/10/34.**G.**
Gor. 31/12/35—25/1/36.**G.**
Gor. 29/5—19/6/37.**G.**
Gor. 11/2—18/3/39.**G.**
Gor. 5—26/10/40.**G.**
Gor. 12/12/42—30/1/43.**G.**
Four new cylinders fitted.
Gor. 12/1—5/2/44.**G.**
Gor. 11/5—22/6/46.**G.**

BOILERS:
1930.
1928 *(ex5462)* 28/7/28.
1931 *(ex5031)* 22/11/30.
1922 *(ex5467)* 4/3/33.
　791 *(new)* 27/10/34.
　69 *(ex5037)* 25/1/36.
　583 *(exB8 5440)* 19/6/37.
　77 *(ex5034)* 26/10/40.
3026 *(ex5467)* 30/1/43.
3039 *(exB8 5443)* 5/2/44.
　631 *(ex5032)* 22/6/46.

SHEDS:
Neasden 9/12/21.
Woodford 12/1/23.
Annesley 5/9/43.
Gorton 30/10/43.
Darnall 20/10/46.

RENUMBERED:
5464 26/4/24.
1372 21/7/46.

CONDEMNED: 10/9/48.
Cut up at Dukinfield.

5465

Gorton.

To traffic 8/1921.

REPAIRS:
Gor. 22/3—24/5/24.**G.**
Gor. 10/4—10/7/26.**G.**
Gor. 15/10—10/12/27.**G.**
Gor. 30/3—18/5/29.**G.**
Gor. 14/9—19/10/29.**G.**
Gor. 25/4—23/5/31.**G.**
Gor. 20/5—17/6/33.**G.**
Gor. 9/2—2/3/35.**G.**
Gor. 10—31/10/36.**G.**
Gor. 8—29/10/38.**G.**
Gor. 26/8—14/10/39.**G.**
New inside cylinders fitted.
Gor. 1/2—1/3/41.**G.**
Gor. 2—24/4/43.**G.**
Gor. 10—28/10/44.**G.**

WORKS CODES:- Cw - Cowlairs. Dar- Darlington. Don - Doncaster. Ghd - Gateshead. Gor - Gorton. Inv - Inverurie. Str - Stratford.
REPAIR CODES:- **C/H** - Casual Heavy. **C/L** - Casual Light. **G** - General. **H**- Heavy. **H/I** - Heavy Intermediate. **L** - Light. **L/I** - Light Intermediate. **N/C** - Non-Classified.

91

5465 continued.
Gor. 4/8—15/9/45.**G.**
New inside cylinders fitted.
Gor. 26/4—31/5/47.**G.**

BOILERS:
77.
1922 *(ex5037)* 10/12/27.
1921 *(ex5072)* 23/5/31.
59 *(ex5474)* 17/6/33.
631 *(exB8 5446)* 2/3/35.
65 *(exB3 6168)* 31/10/36.
3005 *(exB3 6165)* 29/10/38.
3026 *(new)* 14/10/39.
267 *(ex5462)* 1/3/41.
3022 *(exB8 5444)* 24/4/43.
3040 *(exB8 5279)* 28/10/44.
3003 *(ex1365)* 31/5/47.

SHEDS:
Sheffield 24/2/22.
Gorton 24/5/24.
Sheffield 5/6/24.
Gorton 10/2/26.
Woodford 11/10/35.
Gorton 30/10/43.

RENUMBERED:
5465 24/5/24.
1373 14/9/46.

CONDEMNED: 19/8/48.
*Into Gor. for cut up 21/8/48 but
cut up at Dukinfield.*

5466

Gorton.

To traffic 10/1921.

REPAIRS:
Gor. 5/4—5/7/24.**G.**
Gor. 28/8—4/12/26.**G.**
Gor. 5/1—2/3/29.**G.**
Gor. 9/8—27/9/30.**G.**
Gor. 18/6—16/7/32.**G.**
Gor. 14/4—26/5/34.**G.**
Gor. 7/3—4/4/36.G.
Gor. 22/1—19/2/38.**G.**
Gor. 15/6—6/7/40.**G.**
Gor. 7/10—8/11/41.**G.**
Four new cylinders fitted.
Gor. 20/12/41—17/1/42.**L.**
After collision.
Gor. 25/11—18/12/43.**G.**
Gor. 26/1—23/3/46.**G.**
Gor. 18/9/48. *Not repaired.*

BOILERS:
80.
73 *(ex5036)* 2/3/29.
356 *(ex5484)* 27/9/30.
1848 *(ex5078)* 16/7/32.
1928 *(exB2 5426)* 26/5/34.

3001 *(exB2 5427)* 4/4/36.
3020 *(new)* 19/2/38.
631 *(exB3 6165)* 6/7/40.
3024 *(ex5478)* 8/11/41.
3029 *(ex5470)* 18/12/43.

SHEDS:
Sheffield 24/2/22.
Neasden 9/9/25.
Gorton 5/3/29.
Neasden 30/3/29.
Woodford 9/2/41.
Gorton 30/10/43.

RENUMBERED:
5466 5/7/24.
1374 15/11/46.

CONDEMNED: 18/9/48.
Cut up at Dukinfield.

5467

Gorton.

To traffic 2/1922.

REPAIRS:
Gor. 5/1—15/3/24.**G.**
Gor. 10/4—30/6/26.**G.**
Gor. 15/10—3/12/27.**G.**
Gor. 11/5—29/6/29.**G.**
Gor. 25/4—30/5/31.**G.**
Gor. 14/1—4/2/33.**G.**
Gor. 9—30/3/35.**G.**
Gor. 14/3—4/4/36.**G.**
Gor. 16/10—6/11/37.**G.**
Gor. 22/4—20/5/39.**G.**
Gor. 22/3—26/4/41.**G.**
Gor. 5/12/42—9/1/43.**G.**
Gor. 5/5—9/6/45.**G.**
Gor. 18/1—1/3/47.**G.**
Gor. 15/11—20/12/47.**H.**
Four new cylinders fitted.

BOILERS:
160.
1847 *(exB3 6167)* 30/6/26.
1922 *(ex5465)* 30/5/31.
1926 *(exB2 5426)* 4/2/33.
3003 *(new)* 30/3/35.
81 *(exB3 6167)* 4/4/36.
3017 *(new)* 6/11/37.
3004 *(exB3 6164)* 20/5/39.
3026 *(ex5465)* 26/4/41.
3020 *(ex5038)* 9/1/43.
571 *(exB2 5423)* 9/6/45.
3018 *(ex1390)* 1/3/47.

SHEDS:
Woodford 14/7/22.
Gorton 30/6/26.
Woodford 14/9/26.
Neasden 14/1/28.
Immingham 16/7/29.

Woodford 3/5/43.
Annesley 24/5/43.
Woodford 21/6/43.
Annesley 5/7/43.
Gorton 30/10/43.

RENUMBERED:
5467 15/3/24.
1375 28/9/46.
61704 30/4/49.

CONDEMNED: 13/6/49.
Cut up at Dukinfield.

5468

Gorton.

To traffic 3/1922.

REPAIRS:
Gor. 2/2—12/4/24.**G.**
Gor. 19/6—25/9/26.**G.**
Gor. 5/5—1/9/28.**G.**
Gor. 5/4—17/5/30.**G.**
Gor. 17/10—14/11/31.**G.**
Gor. 1—22/4/33.**G.**
Gor. 14/4—16/6/34.**G.**
Gor. 27/7—24/8/35.**G.**
Gor. 25/1—28/3/36.**H.**
Four new cylinders fitted.
Gor. 2—30/10/37.**G.**
Gor. 25/11—9/12/39.**G.**
Gor. 6/7—15/8/42.**G.**
Gor. 2—4/9/43.**L.**
Gor. 1/7—5/8/44.**G.**
Gor. 29/9/45.**L.**
Gor. 24/8—21/9/46.**G.**

BOILERS:
263.
267 *(ex5469)* 1/9/28.
576 *(new)* 14/11/31.
1845 *(ex5481)* 22/4/33.
928 *(new)* 16/6/34.
6 *(exB8 5004)* 30/10/37.
3015 *(ex5461)* 9/12/39.
3021 *(ex5036)* 15/8/42.
3002 *(exB3 6168)* 5/8/44.
3027 *(ex5460)* 21/9/46.

SHEDS:
Woodford 14/7/22.
Neasden 9/10/35.
Woodford 9/2/41.
Gorton 30/10/43.

RENUMBERED:
5468 12/4/24.
1376 21/9/46.

CONDEMNED: 31/12/48.
Cut up at Dukinfield.

5469

Gorton.

To traffic 4/1922.

REPAIRS:
Gor. 23/2—10/5/24.**G.**
Gor. 30/1—10/4/26.**G.**
Gor. 25/2—21/4/28.**G.**
Gor. 18/1—1/3/30.**G.**
Gor. 1/11/30.**L.**
Gor. 14/11—12/12/31.**G.**
Gor. 16/9—7/10/33.**G.**
Gor. 22/12/34—26/1/35.**G.**
Gor. 10—17/8/35.**L.**
Gor. 17/10—7/11/36.**G.**
Gor. 26/3—30/4/38.**G.**
Gor. 23/9—14/10/39.**G.**
Gor. 30/11/40—11/1/41.**G.**
Four new cylinders fitted.
Gor. 31/7—9/8/41.**L.**
After collision.
Gor. 3—26/9/42.**G.**
Gor. 3/1—5/2/44.**G.**
Gor. 1/9—6/10/45.**G.**
Gor. 21/12/46.**L.**
After collision.
Gor. 11/10—8/11/47.**G.**

BOILERS:
267.
292 *(ex5472)* 21/4/28.
579 *(new)* 12/12/31.
1847 *(ex5463)* 7/10/33.
534 *(ex5460)* 7/11/36.
1932 *(ex5484)* 30/4/38.
3016 *(exB8 5440)* 14/10/39.
1922 *(ex5078)* 11/1/41.
3016 *(ex5462)* 26/9/42.
3034 *(ex5482)* 5/2/44.
3028 *(exB8 5280)* 6/10/45.
3042 *(ex1389)* 8/11/47.

SHEDS:
Woodford 14/7/22.
Immingham 10/5/24.
Gorton 18/7/29.
Neasden 3/5/34.
Gorton 26/9/34.
Annesley 31/10/35.
Gorton 30/10/43.
Darnall 15/9/46.

RENUMBERED:
5469 10/5/24.
1377 13/11/46.
61705 7/5/49.

CONDEMNED: 13/2/50.
Into Gor. for cut up 18/2/50.

92

On some of the earlier applications of the Gresley valve it was fitted to one end of the header and was then carried on the side of the smokebox. Gorton shed.

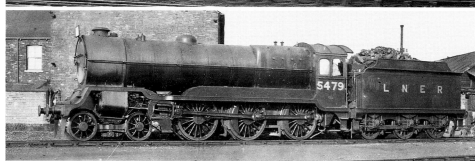

By the middle 1930's all the class had the anti-vacuum valve in normal central position behind the chimney. Hull Botanic Gardens shed.

Two Ross 'pop' safety valves were standard equipment on all the class and from the start, but the mounting of them could vary. According to Diagram they were short type, 3½in diameter and mounted on a rectangular pad. On 3rd May 1941, 5477 was recorded as changed to 3in. diameter but was an odd one.

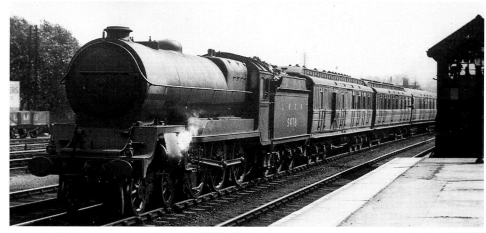

Some of the Part 2 engines when new were fitted with the muffled type of Ross 'pops'. Nos.475, 476, 478 and 481 being known.

All were fitted with ash ejector and on the twenty-eight GCR built engines the steam pipe entered at the back of the smokebox (*see* page 84, second from top), which caused scouring of the front tube plate. The ten Part 2 engines built in 1923/1924 had the steam supply pipe to the ash ejector taken to the front end of the smokebox which avoided affecting the tube plate. This later arrangement was soon adopted for the Part 1 engines, all being so altered by February 1927. Although the ash ejector was still fitted to 1946, they were then removed from the whole class (*see* page 99, centre). Neasden shed.

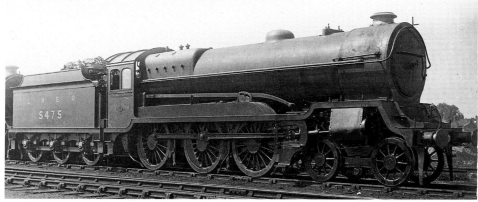

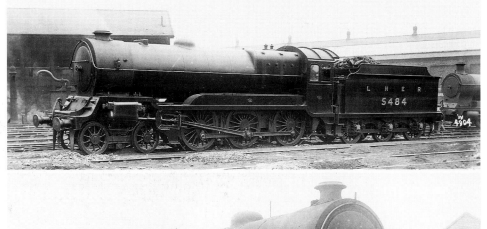

The ten LNER built engines had boiler mountings and cab roof cut down so that no height from rail exceeded 12ft 10¹³⁄₁₆in. and they were within the composite load gauge. The later use of low dome boiler did not affect engines of Part 1 as their chimney and cab heights still exceeded 13ft 0in. Gorton shed.

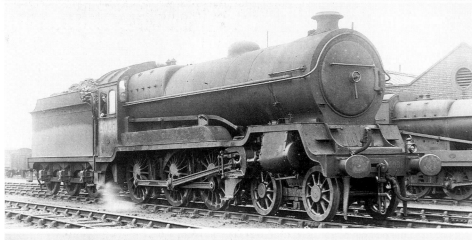

The reversion in 1934/1935 to a GC style of chimney did not require a shortened design unless alteration to the cab roof was also made, and no steps were taken in that direction. Woodford shed.

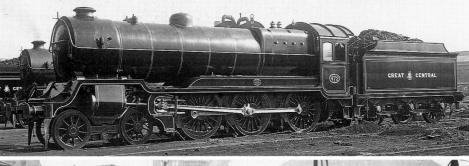

During 1923, No.472 was fitted with a chimney only 10¼in high and this pattern was used for the Part 2 engines. Gorton shed.

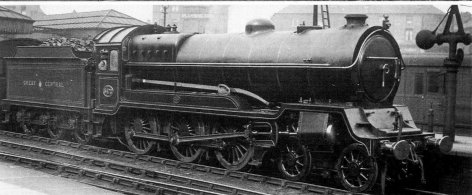

In May 1924, No.5472 changed its chimney again to one of the LNER pattern as used on the new D11/2 class, and also got a lower dome cover, but no alteration was made to the cab so it remained a Part 1 engine. Nottingham (Victoria).

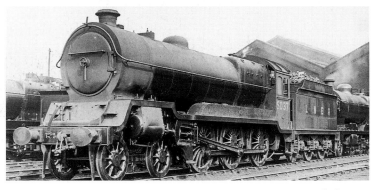

From 1925 on Part 1 engines a gradual change was made to a built-up type of chimney and all twenty-eight engines were so fitted. This chimney was the same height as the one it replaced. Mexborough shed.

5470

Gorton.

To traffic 5/1922.

REPAIRS:
Gor. 27/10/23—16/1/24.**G.**
Gor. 19/12/25—13/3/26.**G.**
Gor. 24/9—19/11/27.**G.**
Gor. 27/7—21/9/29.**G.**
Gor. 13/6—11/7/31.**G.**
Gor. 11/3—8/4/33.**G.**
Gor. 4—25/8/34.**G.**
Gor. 18/4—9/5/36.**G.**
Gor. 12—26/2/38.**G.**
Gor. 23/9—14/10/39.**G.**
Gor. 30/7—23/8/41.**G.**
Gor. 13/10—6/11/43.**G.**
Gor. 27/10—24/11/45.**G.**
Gor. 21/12/46—18/1/47.**L.**
After collision.
Gor. 13/9/47.**L.**

BOILERS:
273.
66 (*ex5478*) 21/9/29.
1846 (*exB3 6166*) 8/4/33.
784 (*new*) 25/8/34.
1928 (*ex5466*) 9/5/36.
263 (*ex5037*) 26/2/38.
3027 (*new*) 14/10/39.
3029 (*ex5477*) 23/8/41.
3012 (*ex5473*) 6/11/43.
583 (*exB8 5440*) 24/11/45.

SHEDS:
Gorton 13/5/22.
Sheffield 21/4/24.
Gorton 5/6/24.
Colwick 4/3/37.
Annesley 5/1/38.
Gorton 6/11/43.
Darnall 15/9/46.

RENUMBERED:
5470 9/2/24.
1378 22/11/46.

CONDEMNED: 19/8/48.
Into Gor. for cut up 21/8/48 but cut up at Darlington 11/48.

5471

Gorton.

To traffic 6/1922.

REPAIRS:
Gor. 9/8—27/9/24.**G.**
Gor. 20/2—1/5/26.**G.**
Gor. 7/4—2/6/28.**G.**
Gor. 11/1—22/2/30.**G.**
Gor. 8/11/30.**L.**

Gor. 21/11—26/12/31.**G.**
Gor. 21/10—18/11/33.**G.**
Gor. 6—27/4/35.**G.**
Gor. 18/7—1/8/36.**G.**
Gor. 4/12/37—8/1/38.**G.**
Gor. 23/12/39—3/2/40.**G.**
Gor. 7—26/9/42.**G.**
Gor. 6/10—13/11/43.**H.**
Four new cylinders fitted.
Gor. 2/3—13/4/46.**G.**
Gor. 21/6—9/8/47.**H.**
New inside cylinders fitted.

BOILERS:
274.
554 (*new*) 27/9/24.
345 (*ex5481*) 26/12/31.
45 (*new*) 18/11/33.
3013 (*new*) 1/8/36.
86 (*ex5035*) 8/1/38.
3019 (*ex5482*) 3/2/40.
3001 (*ex5463*) 26/9/42.

SHEDS:
Gorton 3/6/22.
Sheffield 21/4/24.
Gorton 13/7/24.
Annesley 10/2/32.
Woodford *at* 1/1/35.
Sheffield 8/1/38.
Annesley 3/5/43.
Gorton 13/11/43.
Darnall 15/9/46.

RENUMBERED:
5471 27/9/24.
1379 21/7/46.

CONDEMNED: 12/2/49.
Cut up at Dukinfield.

5472

Gorton.

To traffic 6/1922.

REPAIRS:
Gor. 23/2—3/5/24.**G.**
Gor. 14/11—20/2/26.**G.**
Gor. 29/10—31/12/27.**G.**
Gor. 29/6—10/8/29.**G.**
Gor. 14/11—19/12/31.**G.**
Gor. 27/5—24/6/33.**G.**
Gor. 17/2—3/3/34.**G.**
Gor. 21/9—12/10/35.**G.**
Gor. 13/3—3/4/37.**G.**
Gor. 27/8—24/9/38.**G.**
Gor. 22/6—13/7/40.**G.**
Gor. 26/4—21/6/41.**G.**
Four new cylinders fitted.
Gor. 20/4—8/5/43.**G.**
Gor. 2—23/12/44.**G.**
Gor. 1/3—5/4/47.**G.**
Gor. 3/8/48. *Not repaired.*

BOILERS:
292.
397 (*exB8 5443*) 31/12/27.
1929 (*exB3 6168*) 10/8/29.
1925 (*ex5460*) 19/12/31.
571 (*exB3 6165*) 24/6/33.
1930 (*ex5479*) 3/3/34.
1849 (*ex5459*) 12/10/35.
356 (*exB2 5428*) 3/4/37.
3012 (*ex5474*) 24/9/38.
559 (*ex5458*) 13/7/40.
3018 (*exB8 5439*) 8/5/43.
3037 (*ex5073*) 23/12/44.
571 (*ex1375*) 5/4/47.

SHEDS:
Gorton 24/6/22.
Sheffield 5/5/24.
Gorton 26/12/24.
Annesley 21/7/33.
Gorton 30/10/43.
Darnall 15/9/46.
Gorton 16/4/47.

RENUMBERED:
5472 3/5/24.
1380 15/12/46.

CONDEMNED: 3/8/48.
Cut up at Dukinfield.

5473

Gorton.

To traffic 7/1922.

REPAIRS:
Gor. 23/2—26/4/24.**G.**
Gor. 12/6—4/9/26.**G.**
Gor. 22/9/28—5/1/29.**G.**
Gor. 23/2—2/3/29.**L.**
After collision.
Gor. 16/8—4/10/30.**G.**
Gor. 29/10—19/11/32.**G.**
Gor. 10/11—1/12/34.**G.**
Gor. 21/11—11/12/36.**G.**
Gor. 12/11—10/12/38.**G.**
Gor. 24/8—21/9/40.**G.**
Gor. 11—29/5/43.**G.**
Gor. 31/3—12/5/45.**G.**
Gor. 23/3—6/4/46.**L.**
New L.H. outside cylinder fitted.
Gor. 9/8—6/9/47.**G.**

BOILERS:
295.
534 (*exB3 6166*) 5/1/29.
73 (*ex5466*) 4/10/30.
534 (*ex5035*) 19/11/32.
397 (*ex5032*) 1/12/34.
59 (*exB3 6164*) 11/12/36.
3009 (*ex5481*) 10/12/38.
3012 (*ex5472*) 21/9/40.
784 (*ex5072*) 29/5/43.

3050 (*new*) 6/9/47.

SHEDS:
Gorton 29/7/22.
York 22/9/24.
Gorton 28/2/25.
Neasden 27/1/27.
Immingham 4/3/40.
Lincoln 5/7/42.
Immingham 1/11/42.
Woodford 29/5/43.
Gorton 30/10/43.

RENUMBERED:
5473 26/4/24.
1381 12/1/47.
61706 30/4/49.

CONDEMNED: 26/12/49.
Into Gor. for cut up 31/12/49 but cut up at Dukinfield.

5474

Gorton.

To traffic 8/1922.

REPAIRS:
Gor. 17/5—26/7/24.**G.**
Gor. 25/7—17/10/25.**G.**
Gor. 12/2—16/4/27.**G.**
Gor. 16/2—30/3/29.**G.**
Gor. 31/1—14/3/31.**G.**
Gor. 8/4—6/5/33.**G.**
Gor. 21/7—25/8/34.**G.**
Gor. 13/6—11/7/36.**G.**
Gor. 11/6—2//7/38.**G.**
Gor. 21/9—12/10/40.**G.**
Gor. 2—24/4/43.**G.**
Gor. 9/12/44—6/1/45.**G.**
Gor. 22/2—22/3/47.**G.**

BOILERS:
300.
59 (*ex5477*) 30/3/29.
526 (*new*) 6/5/33.
3012 (*new*) 11/7/36.
534 (*ex5469*) 2/7/38.
3023 (*exB2 5427*) 12/10/40.
1932 (*exB3 6166*) 24/4/43.
81 (*ex5458*) 6/1/45.
3009 (*ex1366*) 22/3/47.

SHEDS:
Gorton 26/8/22.
Neasden 16/6/27.
Woodford 27/9/41.
Gorton 30/10/43.

RENUMBERED:
5474 26/7/24.
1382 1/12/46.
61707 30/4/49.

5474 continued.
CONDEMNED: 13/6/49.
Cut up at Dukinfield.

5031

Beyer, Peacock 6107.

To traffic 7/1922.

REPAIRS:
Gor. 16/12/22—17/2/23.**L.**
After collision.
Gor. 20/9—29/11/24.**G.**
Gor. 23/10/26—8/1/27.**G.**
Gor. 18/8—13/10/28.**G.**
Gor. 5/7—9/8/30.**G.**
Gor. 30/7—20/8/32.**G.**
Gor. 16/12/33—20/1/34.**G.**
Gor. 14/3—4/4/36.**G.**
Gor. 8—29/1/38.**G.**
Gor. 17/8—7/9/40.**G.**
Gor. 17/8—25/9/43.**G.**
Gor. 21/10/44.**L.**
Gor. 22/12/45—26/1/46.**G.**

BOILERS:
1931.
244 (*ex5480*) 9/8/30.
388 (*exB2 5428*) 20/8/32.
273 (*ex5475*) 20/1/34.
3010 (*new*) 4/4/36.
784 (*exB2 5424*) 29/1/38.
576 (*ex5038*) 7/9/40.
3025 (*ex5459*) 25/9/43.
3012 (*ex5470*) 26/1/46.

SHEDS:
Leicester 29/9/22.
Gorton 10/3/23.
Brunswick 9/2/38.
Gorton 11/8/40.
Brunswick 20/9/40.
Annesley 3/5/43.
Gorton 30/10/43.
Darnall 25/6/45.

RENUMBERED:
5031 29/11/24.
1383 2/8/46.

CONDEMNED: 14/5/48.
Into Gor. for cut up 15/5/48 but cut up at Dukinfield.

5032

Beyer, Peacock 6108.

To traffic 7/1922.

REPAIRS:
Gor. 20/12/24—28/2/25.**G.**
Gor. 13/8—8/10/27.**G.**
Gor. 6/7—17/8/29.**G.**

Gor. 18/4—23/5/31.**G.**
Gor. 29/4—20/5/33.**G.**
Gor. 20/10—10/11/34.**G.**
Gor. 25/4—16/5/36.**G.**
Gor. 3—31/7/37.**G.**
Gor. 4/2—4/3/39.**G.**
Gor. 21/9—12/10/40.**G.**
Gor. 21/2—28/3/42.**G.**
Gor. 24/2—25/3/44.**G.**
Gor. 16/2—30/3/46.**G.**
Gor. 31/1/48.**L.**
Firehole ring fracture.

BOILERS:
1932.
1923 (*ex5037*) 23/5/31.
397 (*ex5037*) 20/5/33.
1931 (*ex5072*) 10/11/34.
1846 (*B8 5442*) 16/5/36.
267 (*ex5072*) 31/7/37.
791 (*ex5072*) 4/3/39.
3009 (*ex5473*) 12/10/40.
3033 (*new*) 28/3/42.
631 (*ex5037*) 25/3/44.
3030 (*ex5481*) 30/3/46.

SHEDS:
Leicester 29/9/22.
Annesley 19/7/24.
Leicester 15/11/24.
Gorton 24/2/25.
Leicester 8/6/25.
Neasden 7/10/27.
Gorton 22/10/27.
Sheffield 17/2/28.
Gorton 29/6/29.
Annesley 3/2/34.
Gorton 30/10/43.
Darnall 25/6/45.

RENUMBERED:
5032 28/2/25.
1384 20/12/46.

CONDEMNED: 19/8/48.
Into Gor. for cut up 21/8/48 but cut up at Dukinfield.

5033

Beyer, Peacock 6109.

To traffic 8/1922.

REPAIRS:
Gor. 27/6—26/9/25.**G.**
Gor. 27/8—29/10/27.**G.**
Gor. 4/5—8/6/29.**G.**
Gor. 21/2—21/3/31.**G.**
Gor. 15/4—6/5/33.**G.**
Gor. 4—25/8/34.**G.**
Gor. 6—20/10/34.**L.**
Lubricator changed.
Gor. 30/5—27/6/36.**G.**
Gor. 7/8—25/9/37.**G.**

Four new cylinders fitted.
Gor. 28/10—18/11/39.**G.**
Gor. 17/3—11/4/42.**G.**
Gor. 15/1—6/3/43.**L.**
After collision.
Gor. 10/3—8/4/44.**G.**
Gor. 3—24/8/46.**G.**

BOILERS:
1933.
295 (*ex5473*) 8/6/29.
66 (*ex5470*) 6/5/33.
781 (*new*) 25/8/34.
1931 (*ex5032*) 27/6/36.
3005 (*ex5465*) 18/11/39.
3014 (*exB8 5004*) 11/4/42.
3026 (*ex5464*) 8/4/44.
3048 (*new*) 24/8/46.

SHEDS:
Leicester 5/8/22.
Annesley 19/7/24.
Gorton 8/6/25.
Sheffield 16/2/28.
Gorton 6/5/29.
Sheffield 29/6/29.
Annesley 3/5/43.
Gorton 30/10/43.
Darnall 25/6/45.
Gorton 16/4/47.

RENUMBERED:
5033 26/9/25.
1385 1/12/46.

CONDEMNED: 12/1/49.
Into Gor. for cut up 15/1/49 but cut up at Dukinfield.

5034

Beyer, Peacock 6110.

To traffic 8/1922.

REPAIRS:
Gor. 7/5—26/7/24.**G.**
Gor. 23/10—15/1/27.**G.**
Gor. 31/12/27—11/2/28.**G.**
Gor. 3/11—29/12/28.**G.**
Gor. 25/10—6/12/30.**G.**
Gor. 8/10—5/11/32.**G.**
Gor. 18/8—15/9/34.**G.**
Gor. 15/8—5/9/36.**G.**
Gor. 12/11—10/12/38.**G.**
Gor. 21/9—19/10/40.**G.**
Gor. 30/9—14/11/42.**G.**
Gor. 18/9—14/10/44.**G.**
Gor. 8/2—22/3/47.**G.**

BOILERS:
1934.
1928 (*ex5464*) 6/12/30.
355 (*exB3 6168*) 5/11/32.
66 (*ex5033*) 15/9/34.

3002 (*exB8 5446*) 5/9/36.
77 (*exB8 5279*) 10/12/38.
791 (*ex5032*) 19/10/40.
3006 (*ex5476*) 14/11/42.
928 (*ex5476*) 14/10/44.
3021 (*exB2 1492*) 22/3/47.

SHEDS:
Gorton 25/8/22.
Sheffield 19/4/24.
Gorton 5/5/24.
Leicester 8/6/25.
Colwick 30/11/25.
Gorton 27/3/26.
Colwick 16/3/37.
Sheffield 13/12/37.
Immingham 17/3/39.
Woodford 3/5/43.
Annesley 24/5/43.
Woodford 21/6/43.
Annesley 5/7/43.
Gorton 24/10/43.
Darnall 25/6/45.

RENUMBERED:
5034 26/7/24.
1386 30/6/46.
61708 *allocated.*

CONDEMNED: 13/6/49.
Cut up at Dukinfield.

5035

Beyer, Peacock 6111.

To traffic 8/1922.

REPAIRS:
Gor. 11/10—29/11/24.**G.**
Gor. 31/11/26—5/2/27.**G.**
Gor. 3/11/28—12/1/29.**G.**
Gor. 18/1/30.**L.**
Gor. 30/8—18/10/30.**G.**
Gor. 1—22/10/32.**G.**
Gor. 14/7—11/8/34.**G.**
Gor. 15/2—7/3/36.**G.**
Gor. 27/11—18/12/37.**G.**
Gor. 23/12/39—20/1/40.**G.**
Gor. 13/2—14/3/42.**G.**
Gor. 20/12/43—22/1/44.**G.**
After collision.
Gor. 27/10—24/11/45.**H.**
Firebox fracture.
Gor. 27/12/47—31/1/48.**G.**

BOILERS:
1935.
274 (*ex5471*) 29/11/24.
534 (*ex5473*) 18/10/30.
263 (*ex5036*) 22/10/32.
354 (*ex5036*) 11/8/34.
86 (*exB8 5439*) 7/3/36.
3018 (*new*) 18/12/37.
3013 (*ex5477*) 20/1/40.

5035 continued.
3030 *(exB2 5428)* 14/3/42.
  51 *(ex5460)* 22/1/44.
3034 *(ex5469)* 24/11/45.
3040 *(ex1373)* 31/1/48.

SHEDS:
Gorton 1/9/22.
Annesley 10/6/25.
Gorton 17/4/26.
Neasden 14/2/29.
Gorton 23/3/29.
Immingham 30/8/40.
Lincoln 5/7/42.
Immingham 1/11/42.
Woodford 3/5/43.
Annesley 24/5/43.
Woodford 21/6/43.
Annesley 5/7/43.
Gorton 30/10/43.
Darnall 25/6/45.

RENUMBERED:
  5035 29/11/24.
  1387 8/12/46.
  ᴇ1387 31/1/48.
  61709 7/5/49.

CONDEMNED: 9/1/50.
Into Gor. for cut up 14/1/50.

5475

Gorton.

To traffic 11/8/23.

REPAIRS:
Gor. 19/9—12/12/25.**G.**
Gor. 17/9—5/11/27.**G.**
Gor. 5/10—30/11/29.**G.**
Gor. 23/1—13/2/32.**G.**
Gor. 9/12/33—6/1/34.**G.**
Gor. 10—31/8/35.**G.**
Gor. 1—22/5/37.**G.**
Gor. 22/1—5/2/38.**L.**
After collision.
Gor. 11/2—18/3/39.**G.**
Gor. 9/6—12/7/41.**G.**
Gor. 25/5—19/6/43.**G.**
Gor. 22/7—5/8/44.**L.**
Gor. 25/8—22/9/45.**G.**
Gor. 18/10—22/11/47.**G.**

BOILERS:
  499.
  406 *(exB3 6164)* 30/11/29.
  273 *(ex5482)* 13/2/32.
  554 *(ex5038)* 6/1/34.
3007 *(new)* 31/8/35.
  554 *(ex5038)* 22/5/37.
3028 *(ex5484)* 12/7/41.
  559 *(ex5472)* 19/6/43.
3020 *(ex5467)* 22/9/45.
3022 *(ex1361)* 22/11/47.

SHEDS:
Neasden 11/8/23.
Gorton 10/12/25.
Doncaster 25/3/34.
Gorton 8/9/34.
Lincoln 9/10/35.
Gorton 5/11/35.
Immingham 30/8/40.
Gorton 24/10/43.
LM Region 12/6/49.
Gorton 24/6/49.

RENUMBERED:
  475ᴄ *as new.*
  5475 12/12/25.
  1388 19/12/46.
  61710 14/5/49.

CONDEMNED: 20/2/50.
Into Gor. for cut up 25/2/50.

5476

Gorton.

To traffic 25/8/23.

REPAIRS:
Gor. 5/9—5/12/25.**G.**
Gor. 1/10—26/11/27.**G.**
Gor. 17/8—5/10/29.**G.**
Gor. 14/11—19/12/31.**G.**
Gor. 10/6—8/7/33.**G.**
Gor. 25/5—22/6/35.**G.**
Gor. 26/10—23/11/35.**G.**
Gor. 8/5—5/6/37.**G.**
Gor. 26/11—17/12/38.**G.**
Gor. 28/1—4/2/39.**L.**
Gor. 1—22/6/40.**G.**
After collision.
Gor. 29/8—26/9/42.**G.**
Don. 12/4—22/5/43.**L.**
Gor. 22/7—12/8/44.**G.**
Gor. 15/2—22/3/47.**G.**

BOILERS:
  503.
1933 *(ex5033)* 5/10/29.
1921 *(ex5465)* 8/7/33.
3005 *(new)* 22/6/35.
  763 *(ex5477)* 23/11/35.
3007 *(ex5475)* 5/6/37.
  59 *(ex5473)* 17/12/38.
3006 *(ex5036)* 22/6/40.
  928 *(exB8 5442)* 26/9/42.
3042 *(new)* 12/8/44.
3031 *(ex1396)* 22/3/47.

SHEDS:
Neasden.
Gorton 1/12/25.
Immingham 1/1/36.
Gorton 29/6/38.
Annesley 19/5/43.
Gorton 30/10/43.

RENUMBERED:
  476ᴄ *as new.*
  5476 5/12/25.
  1389 20/10/46.

CONDEMNED: 4/2/49.
Into Gor. for cut up 5/2/49 but cut up at Dukinfield.

5477

Gorton.

To traffic 22/9/23.

REPAIRS:
Gor. 22/8—21/11/25.**G.**
Gor. 20/8—15/10/27.**G.**
Gor. 22/9—22/12/28.**G.**
Gor. 19/7—23/8/30.**G.**
Gor. 8—29/10/32.**G.**
Gor. 30/6—14/7/34.**G.**
Gor. 28/9—19/10/35.**G.**
Gor. 4/7—8/8/36.**L.**
Gor. 25/12/37—22/1/38.**G.**
Gor. 4—25/11/39.**G.**
Gor. 5/4—3/5/41.**H.**
Gor. 31/8—2/10/43.**G.**
Gor. 31/3—28/4/45.**G.**
Gor. 30/11—28/12/46.**H.**
One R.H. cylinder replaced.

BOILERS:
  59.
1927 *(ex5078)* 22/12/28.
  242 *(exB8 5279)* 29/10/32.
  763 *(new)* 14/7/34.
  345 *(ex5038)* 19/10/35.
3013 *(ex5471)* 22/1/38.
3029 *(new)* 25/11/39.
  45 *(exB8 5279)* 3/5/41.
  576 *(ex5031)* 2/10/43.
3018 *(ex5472)* 28/4/45.
3036 *(ex1392)* 28/12/46.

SHEDS:
Gorton.
Neasden *by* 28/6/24.
Immingham 19/11/25.
Gorton 27/6/27.
Immingham 5/1/36.
Lincoln 5/7/42.
Immingham 9/8/42.
Woodford 3/5/43.
Annesley 24/5/43.
Woodford 21/6/43.
Annesley 5/7/43.
Gorton 24/10/43.

RENUMBERED:
  477ᴄ *as new.*
  5477 21/11/25.
  1390 22/11/46.

CONDEMNED: 2/11/48.
Into Gor. for cut up 6/11/48 but cut up at Dukinfield.

5478

Gorton.

To traffic 20/10/23.

REPAIRS:
Gor. 2/5—25/7/25.**G.**
Gor. 30/6—20/8/27.**G.**
Gor. 16/3—20/4/29.**G.**
Gor. 31/1—7/3/31.**G.**
Gor. 26/9—10/10/31.**L.**
Gor. 1/4—6/5/33.**G.**
Gor. 4/1—1/2/36.**G.**
Gor. 9—30/10/37.**G.**
Gor. 15/7—19/8/39.**G.**
Gor. 22/8—18/10/41.**G.**
Gor. 27/10—4/12/43.**G.**
Gor. 26/8/44.**L.**
Gor. 9/12/44.**L.**
Tender in collision.
Gor. 23/6—4/8/45.**G.**
After collision.
Gor. 7—28/2/48.**G.**

BOILERS:
  66.
  69 *(exB3 6167)* 20/4/29.
  576 *(ex5468)* 6/5/33.
3009 *(new)* 1/2/36.
  773 *(exB3 6165)* 30/10/37.
3024 *(new)* 19/8/39.
3027 *(ex5470)* 18/10/41.
3004 *(ex5484)* 4/12/43.
3010 *(exB8 5445)* 4/8/45.
3028 *(ex1377)* 28/2/48.

SHEDS:
Gorton.
Immingham 19/7/29.
Woodford 3/5/43.
Annesley 24/5/43.
Woodford 21/6/43.
Annesley 5/7/43.
Gorton 30/10/43.

RENUMBERED:
  478ᴄ *as new.*
  5478 25/7/25.
  1391 25/11/46.
  ᴇ1391 28/2/48.
  61391 29/1/49.
  61711 30/4/49.

CONDEMNED: 3/7/50.
Into Gor. for cut up 8/7/50.

From 1934/1935 all the Part 1 engines changed again to a cast type of similar shape and the same height as their original equipment. Woodford shed, December 1935.

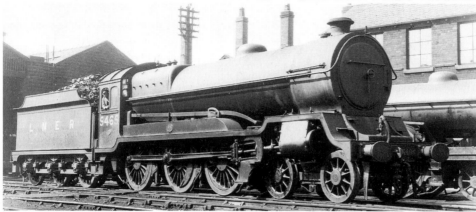

Part 1 engines had the cab front windows shaped at the top to follow the shoulder of the Belpaire firebox.

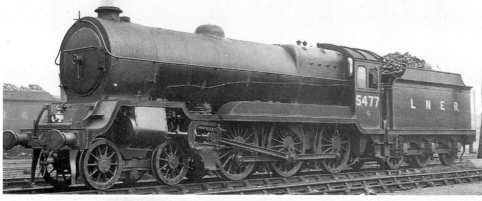

The cab front windows on Part 2 were symmetrical due to the lower cab roof. No B7 was ever fitted with glass sight screens on the cab side. The last five Part 1 and all ten Part 2 engines had buffers with a very pronounced oval head to obviate locking on curves.

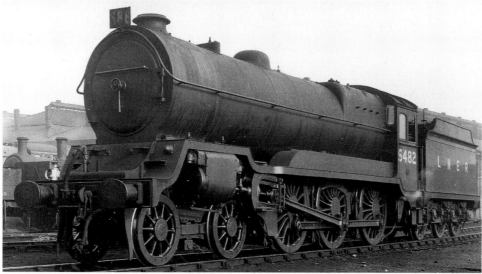

Later there was some interchanging with those which had a more rounded oval head. None were traced as getting GS buffers. Doncaster shed.

All had a heater connection fitted at both ends, but in the summer months often ran without the hose at the front end (*see* page 89, bottom).

The top lamp iron was clamped to the handrail above the door of the smokebox and all kept it there until after the war. Beginning in 1946 this lamp bracket was fitted to the smokebox door to improve access to it, but not all were so altered (*see* page 103, bottom). Dukinfield works.

Putting the lamp bracket on the smokebox door led to some duplications, as here and in the photograph of 5468 on page 86, as the bracket on the handrail was retained. Note new type cylinders and valves, but no provision of relief valves for the outside cylinders. Nos.1378 and 1360 (*see* page 103, bottom), both had two top brackets. The normal smokebox door fastening was by wheel and handle until during the 1939-1945 war.

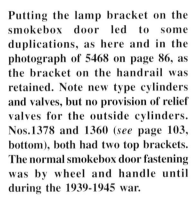

Late in the war period there was a general removal of the wheel which was replaced by a second handle. Lincoln (ex-GN) shed, July 1947.

(bottom) All Part 1 engines originally had black paint with broad red and narrow double white lining. In the spring of 1924 many were still sent out in this livery, as traffic needs precluded repainting after general repairs. The only change was the substitution of the large brass numberplate by one showing the LNER number. No.5460 got this plate on 19th April 1924 but had to wait until 6th March 1926 for its LNER livery. Other B7's treated this way, all in 1924, were: 5462 and 5467 (15th March), 5464 (26th April), 5473 (26th April), 5472 (3rd May), 5469 (10th May), 5036 (17th May) and 5465 (24th May).

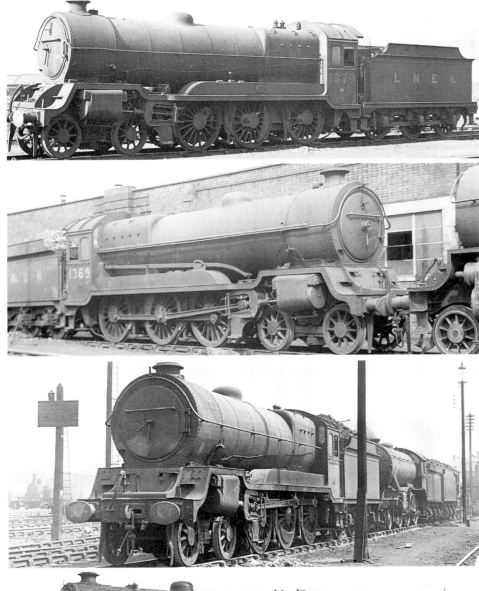

5479

Gorton.

To traffic 3/11/23.

REPAIRS:
Gor. 29/8—14/11/25.**G.**
Gor. 29/10—24/12/27.**G.**
Gor. 31/8—12/10/29.**G.**
Gor. 10/10—14/11/31.**G.**
Gor. 9—23/1/32.**L.**
Gor. 18/11—9/12/33.**G.**
Gor. 10/8—14/9/35.**G.**
Gor. 19/12/36—9/1/37.**G.**
Gor. 6/8—17/9/38.**G.**
Gor. 20/7—10/8/40.**G.**
Gor. 22/10—28/11/42.**G.**
Gor. 21/10—18/11/44.**G.**
Gor. 9/11—7/12/46.**G.**

BOILERS:
 242.
1712 *(exB8 5443)* 12/10/29.
1930 *(exB3 6167)* 14/11/31.
 6 *(exB2 5424)* 9/12/33.
 8 *(exB8 5443)* 14/9/35.
 51 *(ex5461)* 9/1/37.
3014 *(exB3 6168)* 17/9/38.
 59 *(ex5476)* 10/8/40.
 526 *(ex5480)* 28/11/42.
3036 *(exB2 5427)* 18/11/44.
3041 *(ex5037)* 7/12/46.

SHEDS:
Gorton.
Lincoln ?/9/35.
Woodford ?/2/36.
Gorton ?/11/42.
Annesley ?/5/43.
Gorton ?/10/43.

RENUMBERED:
479c *as new.*
5479 14/11/25.
1392 2/11/46.
61712 14/5/49.

CONDEMNED: 13/6/49.
Cut up at Dukinfield.

5480

Gorton.

To traffic 24/11/23.

REPAIRS:
Gor. 25/4—25/7/25.**G.**
Gor. 23/7—17/9/27.**G.**
Gor. 13/10—10/11/28.**L.**
Re-tubing.
Gor. 11/1—22/2/30.**G.**
Gor. 2—23/4/32.**G.**
Gor. 9/12/33—6/1/34.**G.**

Gor. 22/2—14/3/36.**G.**
Gor. 6/11—4/12/37.**G.**
Gor. 9/3—6/4/40.**G.**
Gor. 8/10—7/11/42.**G.**
Gor. 11/11—2/12/44.**G.**
Gor. 28/9—9/11/46.**G.**
New inside cylinders fitted.
Gor. 3/8/48. *Not repaired.*

BOILERS:
 244.
 503 *(ex5476)* 22/2/30.
1849 *(exB3 6165)* 23/4/32.
 300 *(exB8 5443)* 6/1/34.
1845 *(exB2 5425)* 14/3/36.
 81 *(ex5467)* 4/12/37.
 526 *(ex5037)* 6/4/40.
3019 *(ex5471)* 7/11/42.
 526 *(ex5479)* 2/12/44.
3026 *(ex5033)* 9/11/46.

SHEDS:
Gorton.
Sheffield 30/6/30.
Annesley 3/5/43.
Gorton 24/10/43.

RENUMBERED:
480c *as new.*
5480 25/7/25.
1393 8/9/46.

CONDEMNED: 3/8/48.
Cut up at Dukinfield.

5481

Gorton.

To traffic 8/12/23.

REPAIRS:
Gor. 12/9—5/12/25.**G.**
Gor. 20/8—15/10/27.**G.**
Gor. 15/6—27/7/29.**G.**
Gor. 26/9—7/11/31.**G.**
Gor. 26/12/31—13/2/32.**L.**
Gor. 11/3—8/4/33.**G.**
Gor. 15/9—6/10/34.**G.**
Gor. 13/6—4/7/36.**G.**
Gor. 6—27/11/37.**G.**
Gor. 29/10—26/11/38.**G.**
Gor. 23/11—21/12/40.**G.**
Gor. 12/11—12/12/42.**G.**
Gor. 13/1—19/2/44.**G.**
*New R.H. outside cylinder fitted
after collision.*
Gor. 12/1—16/2/46.**G.**

BOILERS:
 345.
1845 *(ex5461)* 7/11/31.
1932 *(exB3 6167)* 8/4/33.
 355 *(ex5034)* 6/10/34.
3011 *(new)* 4/7/36.

3009 *(ex5478)* 27/11/37.
 51 *(ex5479)* 26/11/38.
3041 *(new)* 12/12/42.
3030 *(ex5035)* 19/2/44.
3025 *(ex5031)* 16/2/46.

SHEDS:
Gorton.
Neasden 28/10/27.
Woodford 14/1/28.
Neasden 17/12/29.
Woodford 15/3/30.
Sheffield 7/3/38.
Annesley 3/5/43.
Gorton 30/10/43.

RENUMBERED:
1394 21/9/46.

CONDEMNED: 22/4/48.
*Into Gor. for cut up 24/4/48 but
cut up at Dukinfield.*

5482

Gorton.

To traffic 22/12/23.

REPAIRS:
Gor. 17/10—19/12/25.**G.**
Gor. 26/11/27—28/1/28.**G.**
Gor. 11/1—15/2/30.**G.**
Gor. 19/12/31—23/1/32.**G.**
Gor. 22/7—12/8/33.**G.**
Gor. 5/1—2/2/35.**G.**
Gor. 27/6—25/7/36.**G.**
Gor. 25/12/37—22/1/38.**G.**
Gor. 2—23/12/39.**G.**
Gor. 18/3—11/4/42.**G.**
Gor. 28/12/43—22/1/44.**G.**
Gor. 30/3—27/4/46.**G.**
Gor. 30/11/48. *Not repaired.*

BOILERS:
 354.
 273 *(ex5470)* 15/2/30.
 292 *(ex5469)* 23/1/32.
 559 *(new)* 12/8/33.
 526 *(ex5474)* 25/7/36.
3019 *(new)* 22/1/38.
 244 *(ex5484)* 23/12/39.
3034 *(new)* 11/4/42.
3024 *(ex5466)* 22/1/44.
 763 *(ex5484)* 27/4/46.

SHEDS:
Gorton.
Immingham 3/5/24.
Gorton 17/12/25.
Woodford 18/10/35.
Gorton 30/10/43.
Walton-on-the-Hill 19/1/47.
Gorton 9/2/47.

RENUMBERED:
1395 2/11/46.

CONDEMNED: 30/11/48.
Cut up at Dukinfield.

5483

Gorton.

To traffic 2/2/24.

REPAIRS:
Gor. 10/10—31/12/25.**G.**
Gor. 7/5—30/6/27.**G.**
Gor. 2/3—13/4/29.**G.**
Gor. 15/11—20/12/30.**G.**
Gor. 14/1—4/2/33.**G.**
Gor. 15/12/34—19/1/35.**G.**
Gor. 9—30/1/37.**G.**
Gor. 15/4—13/5/39.**G.**
Gor. 5—30/5/42.**G.**
Gor. 6/5—17/6/44.**G.**
Gor. 21/4—5/5/45.**L.**
After collision.
Gor. 18/1—22/2/47.**G.**

BOILERS:
 355.
 274 *(ex5035)* 20/12/30.
 73 *(ex5473)* 4/2/33.
 424 *(exB2 5423)* 19/1/35.
 8 *(ex5479)* 30/1/37.
3035 *(new)* 30/5/42.
3031 *(exB2 5424)* 17/6/44.
3006 *(exB8 5442)* 22/2/47.

SHEDS:
Gorton.
Sheffield 8/5/29.
Mexborough 11/2/41.
Annesley 3/5/43.
Gorton 24/10/43.

RENUMBERED:
1396 20/10/46.
61396 19/2/49.
61713 30/4/49.

CONDEMNED: 5/9/49.
Cut up at Dukinfield.

5484

Gorton.

To traffic 1/3/24.

REPAIRS:
Gor. 6/3—5/6/26.**G.**
Gor. 26/11—3/12/27.**L.**
Gor. 18/8—13/10/28.**G.**
Gor. 19/7—23/8/30.**G.**
Gor. 6/8—3/9/32.**G.**
Gor. 4/8—15/9/34.**G.**

Gor. 27/6—18/7/36.**G.**
Gor. 19/3—9/4/38.**G.**
Gor. 4/11—2/12/39.**G.**
New inside cylinders fitted.
Gor. 31/5—28/6/41.**G.**
Gor. 21/10—27/11/43.**G.**
Gor. 18/1—2/3/46.**G.**

BOILERS:
  356.
  499 *(ex5475)* 23/8/30.
  244 *(ex5031)* 3/9/32.
1932 *(ex5072)* 18/7/36.
  244 *(exB3 6164)* 9/4/38.
3028 *(new)* 2/12/39.
3004 *(ex5467)* 28/6/41.
  763 *(exB2 5428)* 27/11/43.
3016 *(exB8 5443)* 2/3/46.

SHEDS:
Gorton.
Immingham 30/5/24.
Gorton 5/6/26.
Sheffield 15/7/29.
Gorton 30/6/30.
Woodford 21/1/37.
Gorton 27/11/43.
Darnall 20/10/46.

RENUMBERED:
1397 10/11/46.

CONDEMNED: 4/6/48.
Into Gor. for cut up 5/6/48 but
cut up at Dukinfield.

___

The first six Part 2 engines got a GC number on their brass plate and the same number under LNER on the tender with the area suffix C added. The last four engines had Nos.5481 to 5484 on plates and tender so did not need the suffix (*see* page 94, top) - the view shows change to LNER small plate, in June 1926. Gorton shed.

(*centre*) **Before the traffic need took precedence over the repainting, 5470 left the paint shop on 9th February 1924 in what became standard LNER livery for the class except for the large brass plate on the cab. 5078 (29th March 1924), 5038 (5th April 1924) and 5468 (26th April 1924) were the only others to get this treatment, in the period when engines were being sent out not repainted. Stalybridge, March 1924.**

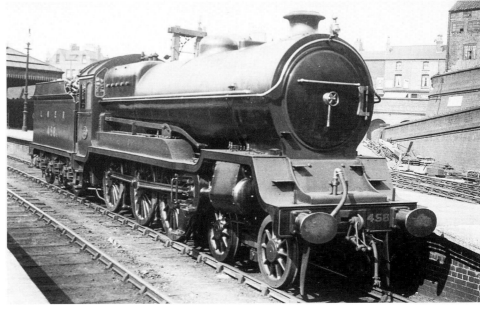

(*right*) **Prior to the February 1924 renumbering, six of the class changed from GCR to LNER livery. After a collision, No.31 was ex paint shop on 3rd March 1923 as L.&N.E.R. The other five got LNER and area suffix C to their number. They were 72c and 458c (3rd November 1923), 73c (24th November 1923), 37c (22nd December 1923) and 459c (19th January 1924). Nottingham (Victoria).**

After the end of May 1924 there were no more number plates of the large GCR type, instead the LNER number plate was fitted. All subsequently got or changed to this small LNER plate. On the tender LNER surmounted the four-figure number and eight went straight to this style: 5461 and 5466 (5th July 1924), 5034 and 5474 (26th July 1924), 5471 (27th September 1924), 5035 (29th November 1924), 5032 (28th February 1925) and 5033 (26th September 1925). The last into this standard style was 5036 on 30th October 1926 which had been given a general repair in May 1924 and renumbered but turned out still in GCR livery.

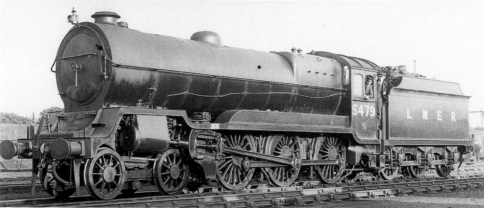

The considerable amount of passenger work done by B7 class qualified them for mixed traffic status so they retained the red lining after the economies of June 1928. From March 1929 the number was moved to the cab side and the LNER on the tender became 12in. instead of 7½in. No.5034, on 6th December 1930, was the last to get a cab number.

In the later 1930's not all got the red lining although the front buffer beam was still lined and panelled. Nottingham (Victoria).

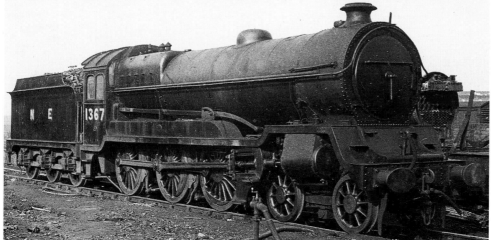

From July 1942 only NE was put on the tender and by then only unlined black was standard and remained so to withdrawal. Gorton works.

Beginning in January 1946, LNER was restored on the tender and for most of that year Gorton continued to use shaded transfers for letters and numbers. No.1390 was one of the last ex works, on 28th December 1946, with the shaded transfers. From there on, the stocks of shaded transfers virtually ran out and no replacements were ordered. However, No.1392 was ex works from a general repair some three weeks prior to No.1390, on 7th December 1946, and it had yellow painted and unshaded letters and numbers in Gill sans but with modified 9.

(right) In January and February 1948 three of the Class 1370, 1387 and 1391 received the regional prefix E to their number and E1370 was withdrawn as such but E1387 became 61709 on 7th May 1949 whilst E1391 became 61391 on 29th January 1949 and 61711 on 30th April 1949 (*see* below). The only other to get two BR numbers was 61396 on 19th February 1949, which changed to 61713 on 30th April 1949.

(right) In the 1946 renumbering B7 class took Nos.1360 to 1397 and all acquired these numbers. The large number of Thompson B1 put on order required these numbers to maintain sequence so on 21st April 1949 the surviving B7's were allotted 61702 to 61713. No.1382 was patched to 61707 on 30th April 1949 using the modified 6. It retained Gill sans LNER on its tender from a 22nd March 1947 repair. The use of the modified 6 so late seems a sole aberration. Gorton shed.

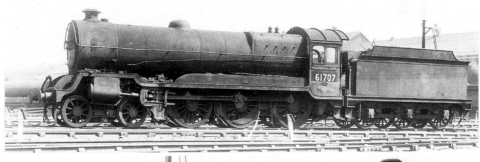

Although 61711 got that number also on 30th April 1949 the correct Gill sans 6 was used and 10in. numbers matched the lettering on the tender. Gorton shed.

After withdrawal in 1948, Nos.1360 (August) and 1378 (September) were sent to Darlington where they were cut up early in November.

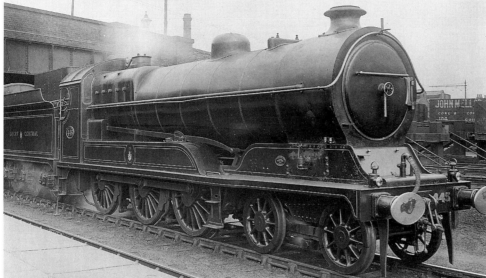

(above) **Ten more engines, Nos.439 to 446, 279 and 280, were built during 1914 and 1915. They were similar to No.4 and were in this condition at Grouping. These ten were fitted with a snifting valve on the frame. Only Nos.439, 446 and 279 were named.**

(left) **Nos.279, 443 and 445 were fitted in 1921 for oil firing and No.445 kept the equipment until it went to works in August 1923. Guide Bridge.**

(left) **All had Robinson type top feed and a smokebox ash ejector, the steam supply pipe for that entering at the rear of the smokebox. The class were built with Ramsbottom safety valves but in October 1920 No.279 was the first to change to Ross 'pop' type. Guide Bridge.**

(below) **Although top feed was being discarded (see page 113, bottom), most still had it when they became LNER engines. Gorton shed.**

CLASS B 8

5004

GLENALMOND

Gorton.

To traffic 6/1913.

REPAIRS:
Gor. 3/11—22/12/17.**G.**
Gor. 19/8—2/9/22.**G.**
Gor. ?/?—3/2/23.*Tender only.*
Gor. 18/4—18/7/25.**G.**
Gor. 22/10—24/12/27.**G.**
New cylinders fitted.
Gor. 29/3—3/5/30.**G.**
Gor. 25/6—16/7/32.**G.**
Gor. 12/11—3/12/32.**L.**
Gor. 29/9—13/10/34.**G.**
Gor. 26/10—23/11/35.**G.**
Gor. 28/8—25/9/37.**G.**
Gor. 23/9/39.**L.**
Superheater header.
Gor. 17/8—7/9/40.**G.**
Gor. 16/2—14/3/42.**G.**
Gor. 22/3—2/5/44.**G.**
Gor. 20/4—8/6/46.**G.**

BOILERS:
1550.
1545 *(exB2 5423)* 22/12/17.
 631 *(ex5280)* 2/9/22.
 354 *(exB7 5482)* 3/5/30.
  77 *(exB2 5423)* 16/7/32.
 263 *(exB7 5035)* 13/10/34.
   6 *(exB7 5479)* 23/11/35.
 571 *(exB7 5459)* 25/9/37.
3014 *(exB7 5479)* 7/9/40.
 773 *(ex5440)* 14/3/42.
3033 *(exB7 5032)* 2/5/44.
3014 *(exB7 5461)* 8/6/46.

SHEDS:
Annesley 3/2/22.
March 1/8/25.
Gorton 29/5/26.
Colwick 9/6/26.
Annesley 8/11/26.
Colwick 16/1/28.
Annesley 15/8/43.
Darnall 27/4/47.

RENUMBERED:
5004 18/7/25.
1349 18/8/46.

CONDEMNED: 28/11/47.
Cut up at Dukinfield

5439

SUTTON NELTHORPE

Gorton.

To traffic 7/1914.

REPAIRS:
Gor. 11/11—30/12/22.**G.**
Gor. 20/6—31/10/25.**G.**
Gor. 16/6—6/10/28.**G.**
Gor. 8/3—26/4/30.**G.**
New cylinders fitted.
Gor. 9/1—13/2/32.**G.**
Gor. 14—28/4/34.**G.**
Gor. 8—22/2/36.**G.**
Gor. 1/8—26/9/36.**G.**
Main frame cracked.
Gor. 20/11—11/12/37.**G.**
Gor. 20/1—10/2/40.**G.**
Gor. 4—27/3/43.**G.**
Gor. 23/6—4/8/45.**G.**

BOILERS:
299.
1550 *(exB2 5427)* 30/12/22.
 305 *(ex5445)* 6/10/28.
  86 *(new)* 28/4/34.
 388 *(ex5280)* 22/2/36.
 928 *(exB7 5468)* 11/12/37.
3018 *(exB7 5035)* 10/2/40.
3008 *(exB2 5425)* 27/3/43.

SHEDS:
Gorton 29/9/22.
Colwick 29/3/26.
Annesley 10/8/43.
Darnall 27/4/47.

RENUMBERED:
439c *after 3/3/23.*
5439 31/10/25.
1350 8/12/46.

CONDEMNED: 14/8/47.
Cut up at Gorton.

5440

Gorton.

To traffic 8/1914.

REPAIRS:
Gor. 25/3—3/6/22.**G.**
New cylinders fitted.
Gor. 28/3—4/7/25.**G.**
Gor. 11/12/26—26/2/27.**G.**
Gor. 8/6—20/7/29.**G.**

Gor. 22/8—17/10/31.**G.**
New cylinders fitted.
Gor. 7/10—4/11/33.**G.**
Gor. 17/8—21/9/35.**G.**
Gor. 8/5—5/6/37.**G.**
Gor. 26/2—26/3/38.**L.**
Cracked frame.
Gor. 2—30/9/39.**G.**
Gor. 24/2—30/3/40.**L.**
After collision.
Gor. 16/10—15/11/41.**G.**
Gor. 1—27/11/43.**G.**
Gor. 30/6—1/9/45.**G.**

BOILERS:
303.
299 *(ex5446)* 4/7/25.
626 *(ex5280)* 17/10/31.
583 *(new)* 4/11/33.
3016 *(new)* 5/6/37.
773 *(exB7 5478)* 30/9/39.
554 *(exB7 5475)* 15/11/41.
583 *(exB7 5078)* 27/11/43.
3004 *(exB7 5478)* 1/9/45.

SHEDS:
Annesley 17/2/22.
Leicester 19/7/24.
Annesley 14/11/24.
March 25/7/25.
Gorton 21/5/26.
Colwick 12/10/27.
Annesley 4/1/33.
Darnall 27/4/47.

RENUMBERED:
5440 4/7/25.
1351 15/9/46.

CONDEMNED: 23/10/47.
Into Gor. for cut up 25/10/47.

5441

Gorton.

To traffic 9/1914.

REPAIRS:
Nea. 5/8—1/9/21.**L.**
Gor. 19/5—28/7/23.**G.**
Gor. 13/6—29/8/25.**G.**
Gor. 5/11/27—14/1/28.**G.**
New cylinders fitted.
Gor. 8/3—26/4/30.**G.**
Gor. 23/7—20/8/32.**G.**
Gor. 17—24/9/32.**L.**
Gor. 1/9—6/10/34.**G.**
Gor. 13/6—4/7/36.**G.**
Gor. 5/11—24/12/38.**G.**

Gor. 1—22/2/41.**G.**
Gor. 29/9—23/10/43.**G.**
Gor. 23/6—25/8/45.**G.**

BOILERS:
305.
626 *(ex5446)* 28/7/23.
630 *(ex5279)* 29/8/25.
1546 *(ex5442)* 20/8/32.
499 *(ex5279)* 6/10/34.
781 *(exB7 5033)* 4/7/36.
556 *(ex5445)* 22/2/41.
781 *(ex5280)* 23/10/43.

SHEDS:
Annesley 6/10/22.
March 3/11/23.
Annesley 25/6/24.
Gorton 9/6/25.
Colwick 27/3/26.
Annesley 9/8/43.

RENUMBERED:
441c 25/8/23.
5441 29/8/25.
1352 17/11/46.

CONDEMNED: 6/5/47.
Into Gor. for cut up 10/5/47.

5442

Gorton.

To traffic 9/1914.

REPAIRS:
Gor. 17/9—8/10/21.**G.**
Gor. 5/1—15/3/24.**G.**
New cylinders fitted.
Gor. 21/11/25—6/2/26.**G.**
Gor. 24/3—12/5/28.**G.**
Gor. 22/3—3/5/30.**G.**
Gor. 28/5—25/6/32.**G.**
Gor. 11—25/2/33.**G.**
New cylinders fitted.
Gor. 29/9—13/10/34.**G.**
Gor. 28/3—25/4/36.**G.**
New cylinders fitted.
Gor. 27/11—18/12/37.**G.**
Gor. 17/2—10/3/40.**G.**
Gor. 23/6—1/8/42.**G.**
Gor. 15—25/9/43.**G.**
New cylinders fitted.
Gor. 10/10—4/11/44.**G.**
Gor. 14/9—9/11/46.**G.**

BOILERS:
309.
1548 *(exB2 5425)* 8/10/21.

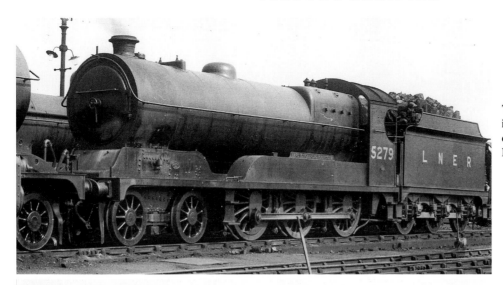

Top feed on B8 actually lasted well into the next decade because No.5279 carried it until September 1932, and No.5439 had it to February 1936.

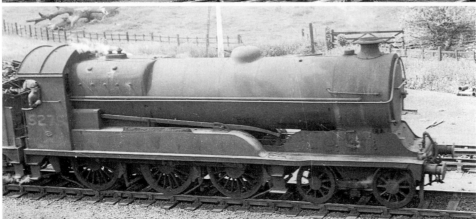

Although the change to Ross 'pop' safety valves began in 1920, the original fitting of four Ramsbottom valves in rectangular brass casing were still in use to June 1925 on No.439. Note addition of Area suffix C to the tender number by Gorton shed although the paint date for L.&N.E.R. was 3rd March 1923. Gorton shed.

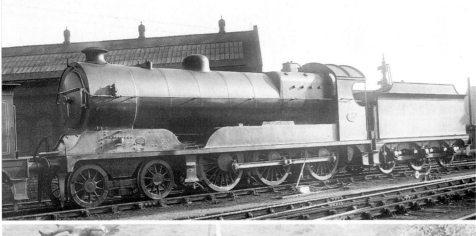

The whole class had Ross 'pops' from 1925 but it was unusual for a casing round the base to be carried. Charwelton, July 1941.

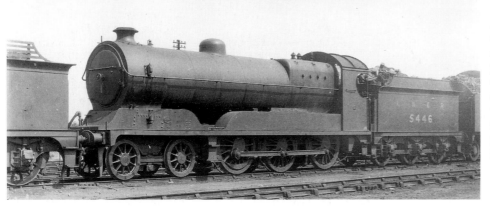

As superheated engines they were equipped with Robinson header discharge valve for element protection. None appear to have carried the combined steam circulating valve and blower control when they became LNER but it is shown on the Gorton official photograph of No.446 when it was new. Annesley shed, June 1926.

After Grouping the header discharge valve was removed but without an alternative being provided in some cases even as late as when 5445 went to works in April 1932. New England shed, July 1931.

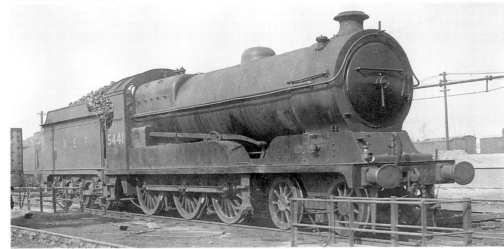

This class were unusually late in being fitted with the Gresley anti-vacuum valve, none being noted whilst the number was still on the tender. They also carried this type on the end of the header later than on other classes. Gorton shed.

No.5441 had a Gresley valve at each end of the header until it went for repair in February 1941. Colwick shed, January 1939.

It was July 1932 before the central position behind the chimney was adopted for the Gresley anti-vacuum valve on B8 class, and it took almost another nine years for all to get it in that standard position.

5442 continued.
599 *(exB3 6169)* 6/2/26.
1546 *(ex5280)* 12/5/28.
1549 *(ex5445)* 25/6/32.
1846 *(exB7 5470)* 13/10/34.
3003 *(exB7 5467)* 25/4/36.
3011 *(exB7 5481)* 18/12/37.
928 *(ex5439)* 10/3/40.
3009 *(exB7 5032)* 1/8/42.
3006 *(exB7 5034)* 4/11/44.
773 *(exB7 5463)* 9/11/46.

SHEDS:
Gorton 27/11/22.
March 10/10/24.
Gorton 22/5/26.
Colwick 9/7/26.
Annesley 15/10/28.
Darnall 27/4/47.

RENUMBERED:
5442 15/3/24.
1353 9/11/46.

CONDEMNED: 24/3/49.
Cut up at Dukinfield

5443

Gorton.

To traffic 10/1914.

REPAIRS:
Gor. 31/7—2/10/20.**G.**
Gor. 13/1—17/2/23.**G.**
Gor. 15/11/24—10/1/25.**G.**
Gor. 9/4—11/6/27.**G.**
Gor. 27/7—14/9/29.**G.**
Gor. 10/10—21/11/31.**G.**
Gor. 16—30/9/33.**G.**
Gor. 22/6—13/7/35.**G.**
Gor. 1—29/2/36.**H.**
New cylinders fitted.
Gor. 1—22/1/38.**G.**
Gor. 4—18/5/40.**G.**
Gor. 11/8—19/9/42.**G.**
Gor. 12/1—4/3/44.**G.**
Gor. 1/12/45—12/1/46.**G.**

BOILERS:
401.
397 *(new)* 17/2/23.
1712 *(exB3 6165)* 11/6/27.
300 *(exB7 5474)* 14/9/29.
8 *(exB2 5427)* 30/9/33.
1921 *(exB7 5476)* 13/7/35.
539 *(ex5444)* 22/1/38.
81 *(exB7 5480)* 18/5/40.
3039 *(new)* 19/9/42.
3016 *(exB7 5469)* 4/3/44.

3005 *(exB2 5424)* 12/1/46.

SHEDS:
Gorton 24/2/22.
March 3/11/23.
Gorton 13/10/24.
Annesley 24/1/25.
Colwick 27/3/26.
Annesley 9/8/43.
Darnall 27/4/47.

RENUMBERED:
5443 10/1/25.
1354 10/11/46.

CONDEMNED: 15/3/48.
Cut up at Dukinfield.

5444

Gorton.

To traffic 10/1914.

REPAIRS:
Gor. 18/12/20—5/2/21.**G.**
Gor. 19/5—4/8/23.**G.**
Gor. 25/10/24—10/1/25.**G.**
Gor. 12/2—9/4/27.**G.**
Gor. 24/11/28—19/1/29.**G.**
Gor. 10/1—21/2/31.**G.**
Gor. 24/6—29/7/33.**G.**
Gor. 20/7—17/8/35.**G.**
New cylinders fitted.
Gor. 4/12/37—8/1/38.**G.**
Gor. 23/3—20/4/40.**G.**
Gor. 23/1—20/2/43.**G.**
Gor. 4—20/11/43.**L.**
New cylinders fitted.
Gor. 26/5—7/7/45.**G.**
Gor. 1/3—19/4/47.**G.**

BOILERS:
406.
1549 *(exB2 5428)* 4/8/23.
1547 *(exB2 5427)* 9/4/27.
599 *(ex5442)* 19/1/29.
1925 *(exB7 5472)* 29/7/33.
539 *(exB7 5463)* 17/8/35.
3003 *(ex5442)* 8/1/38.
3022 *(exB3 6168)* 20/4/40.
3011 *(exB7 5073)* 20/2/43.
3023 *(exB2 5426)* 7/7/45.
3049 *(new)* 19/4/47.

SHEDS:
Gorton 24/2/22.
March 3/11/23.
Gorton 13/10/24.
March 8/6/25.
Gorton 16/6/26.

Colwick 16/6/27.
Annesley 12/10/27.
Colwick 2/4/28.
Annesley 15/6/43.
Darnall 27/4/47.

RENUMBERED:
444c 25/8/23.
5444 10/1/25.
1355 18/8/46.

CONDEMNED: 2/9/48.
Into Gor. for cut up 4/9/48 but cut up at Dukinfield.

5445

Gorton.

To traffic 11/1914.

REPAIRS:
Gor. 3/9—22/10/21.**G.**
Gor. 25/8—22/12/23.**G.**
Gor. 22/5—14/8/26.**G.**
Gor. 7/4—26/5/28.**G.**
Gor. 19/4—24/5/30.**G.**
Gor. 23/4—28/5/32.**G.**
Gor. 30/6—28/7/34.**G.**
Gor. 11/7—1/8/36.**G.**
Gor. 1/10—5/11/38.**G.**
New cylinders fitted.
Gor. 28/12/40—18/1/41.**G.**
Gor. 28/9—24/10/42.**G.**
Gor. 31/3—12/5/45.**G.**

BOILERS:
599.
665 *(exB2 5428)* 22/10/21.
305 *(ex5441)* 22/12/23.
1549 *(ex5444)* 26/5/28.
610 *(exB2 5427)* 28/5/32.
242 *(exB7 5477)* 28/7/34.
556 *(exB3 6169)* 1/8/36.
3007 *(exB2 5423)* 18/1/41.
3010 *(exB3 6168)* 24/10/42.
3032 *(exB7 5459)* 12/5/45.

SHEDS:
Gorton 22/7/21.
March 10/10/24.
Gorton 20/5/26.
Woodford 8/6/28.
March 13/7/28.
Colwick 14/11/28.
Annesley 15/8/43.
Darnall 27/4/47.

RENUMBERED:
5445 2/2/24.
1356 25/8/46.

CONDEMNED: 14/8/47.
Cut up at Gorton.

5446

EARL ROBERTS OF KANDAHAR

Gorton.

To traffic 11/1914.

REPAIRS:
Nea. 12/9—15/10/21.**L.**
Gor. 27/1—10/3/23.**G.**
Gor. 11/10—6/12/24.**G.**
Gor. 9/7—27/8/27.**G.**
Gor. 20/7—24/8/29.**G.**
Gor. 29/8—10/10/31.**G.**
Gor. 7/10—11/11/33.**G.**
Gor. 16/2—16/3/35.**G.**
New cylinders fitted.
Gor. 8—29/8/36.**G.**
Gor. 25/6—16/7/38.**G.**
Gor. 11/5—8/6/40.**G.**
Gor. 8—22/3/41.**L.**
Gor. 13/11/42—23/1/43.**G.**
Gor. 10/3—7/4/45.**G.**
Gor. 15/3—3/5/47.**G.**

BOILERS:
626.
299 *(ex5439)* 10/3/23.
665 *(ex5445)* 6/12/24.
1744 *(exB2 5425)* 10/10/31.
631 *(ex5004)* 11/11/33.
3002 *(new)* 16/3/35.
45 *(exB7 5471)* 29/8/36.
354 *(exB7 5458)* 16/7/38.
539 *(ex5443)* 8/6/40.
3007 *(ex5445)* 23/1/43.
3019 *(exB7 5480)* 7/4/45.
928 *(exB7 1386)* 3/5/47.

SHEDS:
Annesley 3/2/22.
March 3/11/23.
Gorton 6/12/24.
Leicester 2/3/25.
Gorton 8/6/25.
Colwick 29/3/26.
Annesley by 6/6/26.
Darnall 5/5/47.

RENUMBERED:
5446 6/12/24.
1357 17/11/46.

CONDEMNED: 23/4/49.
Cut up at Dukinfield.

WORKS CODES:- Cw - Cowlairs. Dar- Darlington. Don - Doncaster. Ghd - Gateshead. Gor - Gorton. Inv - Inverurie. Str - Stratford.
REPAIR CODES:- C/H - Casual Heavy. **C/L** - Casual Light. **G** - General. **H** - Heavy. **H/I** - Heavy Intermediate. **L** - Light. **L/I** - Light Intermediate. **N/C** - Non-Classified.

108

Until October 1934, the main lubrication was by Robinson Intensifore sight feed type which had been fitted about 1917 replacing Wakefield mechanical. Annesley shed, September 1927.

Between October 1934 (Nos.5441 and 5004) and August 1936 (Nos.5445 and 5279) all had Intensifore taken off and replaced by Eureka sight feed with piping from the cab along the left hand side. No.5443 was so changed in July 1935.

Smokebox ash ejector was fitted, on the right hand side as they were superheated engines. Until after grouping the steam supply pipe entered the rear of the smokebox, No.5439 having it there until June 1928. Annesley shed, June 1926.

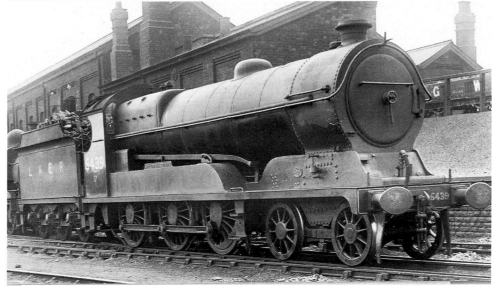

To avoid scouring of the front tube plate which was taking place, the pipe was lengthened so that steam to the ash ejector entered the front end of the smokebox, all were so changed, but not before August 1931 on 5446. Colwick shed.

Although some still had an ash ejector at withdrawal, at least five Nos.1349, 1353, 1355, 1357 and 1358 had it removed in 1946/1947. Doncaster station, December 1946.

In December 1927, No.5004 was fitted with 20in. instead of 21½in. cylinders and was made Part 2 of the class from then on. From June 1927 No.5443 also had 20in. cylinders but in February 1936 regained the normal 21½in. diameter cylinders. Part 2 had no visible difference from Part 1. Sometime during the war it was decided to make other use of the brass wheel which all had as part of the smokebox door fastening.

The wheel was replaced by a second handle by 1945. This photo shows clearly the swivel drawhook with which this class was fitted, and the GCR type buffers, none getting Group Standard type.

5279

EARL KITCHENER OF KHARTOUM

Gorton.

To traffic 12/1914.

REPAIRS:
Gor. 25/9—20/10/20.**G.**
Gor. 23/6—11/8/23.**G.**
Gor. 13/6—5/9/25.**G.**
Gor. 3/12/27—18/2/28.**G.**
Gor. 1/2—1/3/30.**G.**
Gor. 3/9—8/10/32.**G.**
Gor. 25/8—29/9/34.**G.**
Gor. 25/7—15/8/36.**G.**
Gor. 30/7—27/8/38.**G.**
Gor. 5/10—9/11/40.**G.**
Gor. 3/7—8/8/42.**G.**
New cylinders fitted.
Gor. 29/7—19/8/44.**G.**
Gor. 18/5—6/7/46.**G.**

BOILERS:
630.
401 *(ex5443)* 11/8/23.
242 *(exB7 5479)* 1/3/30.
499 *(exB7 5484)* 8/10/32.
295 *(exB3 6165)* 29/9/34.
77 *(exB7 5073)* 15/8/36.
45 *(ex5446)* 27/8/38.
3002 *(exB7 5072)* 9/11/40.
3040 *(new)* 8/8/42.
3043 *(new)* 19/8/44.
3038 *(exB3 6165)* 6/7/46.

SHEDS:
Annesley 3/2/22.
Leicester 19/7/24.
Annesley 6/10/24.
Gorton 8/6/25.
Colwick 31/3/26.
Annesley 8/11/26.
Colwick 6/3/28.
Annesley 9/10/33.
Darnall 27/4/47.

RENUMBERED:
279c 15/9/23.
5279 5/9/25.
1358 25/8/46.

CONDEMNED: 13/8/48.
Into Gor. for cut up 14/8/48 but cut up at Dukinfield.

5280

Gorton.

To traffic 1/1915.

The original chimney was the distinctive Robinson design with a height from rail of 13ft 1¹⁄₁₆in.

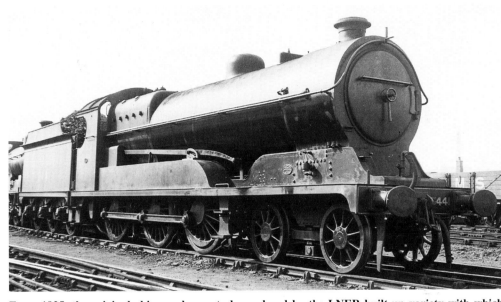

From 1925, the original chimney began to be replaced by the LNER built-up variety with which most of them were fitted. Colwick shed, September 1926.

REPAIRS:
Gor. 7/1—25/2/22.**G.**
Gor. 17/5—19/7/24.**G.**
Gor. 31/12/26—12/3/27.**G.**
Gor. 10/8—21/9/29.**G.**
Gor. 18/7—29/8/31.**G.**
Gor. 20/1—10/2/34.**G.**
Gor. 28/12/35—25/1/36.**G.**
Gor. 13/3—17/4/37.**G.**
Gor. 8/4—6/5/39.**G.**
Gor. 4—30/8/41.**G.**
Gor. 3/7—7/8/43.**G.**
New cylinders fitted.
Gor. 19/5—23/6/45.**G.**
Gor. 26/10/46.**L.**
Firehole ring fracture.

BOILERS:
631.
309 *(ex5442)* 25/2/22.

1546 *(exB2 5424)* 19/7/24.
626 *(ex5441)* 12/3/27.
309 *(exB2 5428)* 29/8/31.
388 *(exB7 5031)* 10/2/34.
274 *(exB2 5426)* 25/1/36.
763 *(exB7 5078)* 6/5/39.
781 *(ex5441)* 30/8/41.
3028 *(exB7 5475)* 7/8/43.
3007 *(ex5446)* 23/6/45.

SHEDS:
Gorton 17/12/22.
March 4/10/24.
Gorton 21/5/26.
Colwick 10/6/26.
Annesley 31/3/27.
Colwick 2/4/28.
Woodford 8/6/28.
March 13/7/28.
Annesley 17/11/28.

RENUMBERED:
5280 19/7/24.
1359 24/11/46.

CONDEMNED: 25/3/47.
Into Gor. for cut up 29/3/47.

111

From 1934/35 there was a further change of chimney and all eleven got a type of cast chimney very similar to their original. Gorton shed, April 1936.

Standard position for the top lamp iron was clamped to the handrail over the smokebox door. But it was unusual to have one there and also one on top of the smokebox. Colwick shed, September 1934.

To improve access to the top lamp bracket some had it transferred on to the smokebox door, in their later days. Nos.1355 and 1357 were so treated but Nos.1349 and 1358 retained it in the original position on the handrail (*see* page 115, top). Gorton shed, March 1948.

Carriage heating connection was provided at both ends of the engine and the tenders had, and retained, water pick-up apparatus. The cab sides were never fitted with hinged glass sight screen and as there was good forward vision through the cab front windows. Nottingham (Victoria).

The original height over the dome cover was 12ft 11¹³⁄₁₆in., but that of the cab was 13ft 1½in. so putting the class outside the composite load gauge. The replacement boilers for the class from 1930 on had low domes as they were also used on B2, B3 and B7 classes to keep within the 13ft 0in. total height in some cases. No effort was ever made to bring the B8's within LNER load gauge.

With their smaller coupled wheels, the GCR classed them as mixed traffic engines and so they got fully lined black livery with a crest on the splasher and on tender. Gorton shed.

Four of the class were early recipients of new livery - on their tender, the engines remaining in the GCR style even including retention of the crest on the splasher. On the tender Great Central and the crest was replaced by 6in. L.&N.E.R. with 12in. numbers below. These four were ex paint shop in 1923 as follows:- No.4 (3rd February), No.439 (3rd March), No.443 (21st April) and No.446 (5th May). The next three got the full LNER style except for keeping the large brass numberplate on the cab. They had single red lining, 7½in. LNER and area suffix C to their 12in. numbers. They were ex paint shop in 1923 as 441c and 444c (25th August) and 279c (15th September). Gorton shed also put suffix C on to L.&N.E.R. 439 at some date not discovered (*see* page 106, second from top). Nottingham (Victoria).

On 2nd February 1924 No.5445 was ex paint shop, the area suffix having been discontinued, and it was fitted with new large brass numberplate 5445 on the cab. Ex works on 15th March 1924 after general repair No.5442 was put into traffic without being repainted but returned to be ex paint shop 24th May 1924 in its LNER livery.

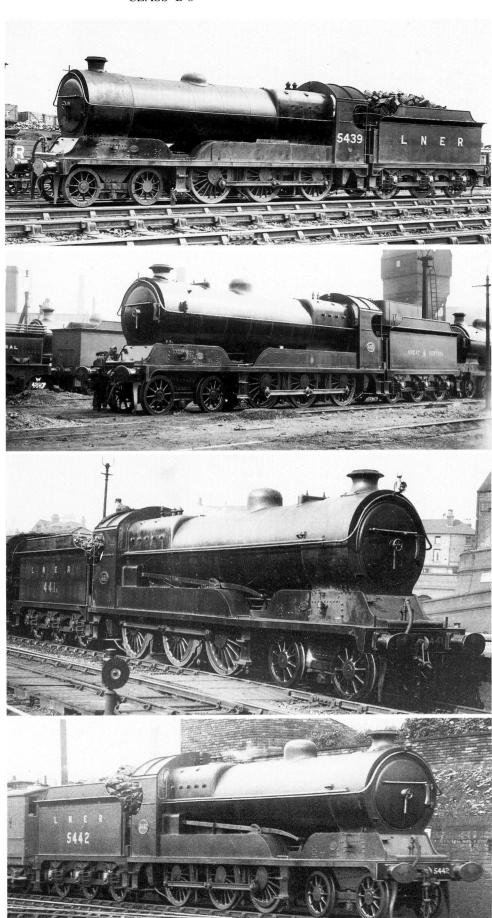

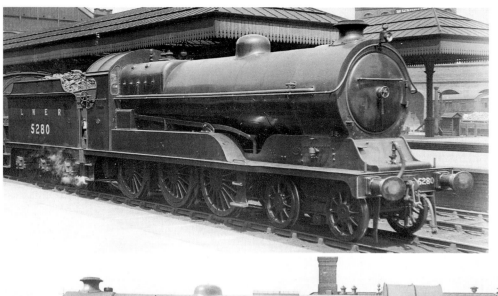

The other two went straight to standard LNER livery with a small numberplate on the cab, No.5280 on 19th July 1924 and 5440 on 4th July 1925. Nottingham (Victoria).

(below) From March 1929, the number was moved to the cab and the LNER on the tender became 12in. At least to 1938 single red lining was still applied. The last B8 to have a tender number was 5444 which went to works in January 1931. Trafford Park shed, August 1936.

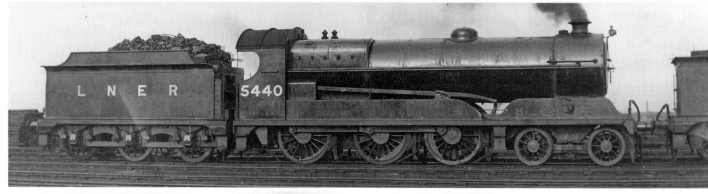

(above) Even before the wartime economies, some B8 class became plain black, the red lining being omitted. Annesley shed, July 1936.

(left) In plain black however, the buffer beam continued to be lined and panelled. From March 1938 a display of the classification was added. Nottingham (Victoria).

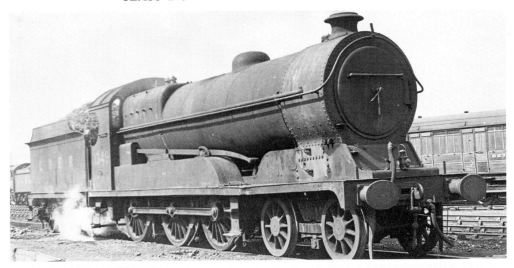

From July 1942 only NE was put on the tender until January 1946 and in that month renumbering began, B8 taking 1349-59. Only five Nos. 1349, 1353, 1355, 1357 and 1358 survived to have LNER again but all five got that, and their new number in shaded transfers. Hull Dairycoates, April 1947.

(above) Annesley based No.441c is seen here in 1924 leaving West Yard at Worksop with an empty wagon train.

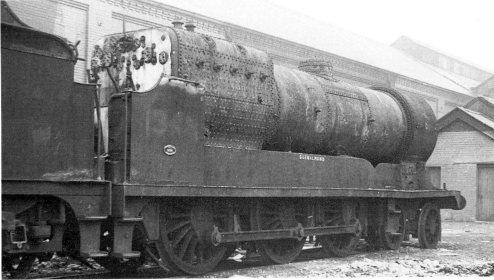

Towards the end of 1947 so many engines which Gorton works maintained were withdrawn that they had to send some to sidings at Dukinfield carriage works to be cut up, and here on 13th March 1948 No.1349 is meeting that fate.

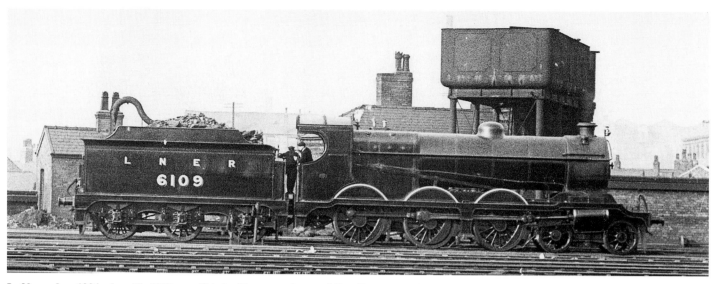

In November 1924 when No.6109 was fitted with a superheater, 21in. diameter cylinders, piston valves and 4in. higher pitched boiler, which was 4ft 9in. diameter against the previous 5ft 0in. diameter boiler. The ash ejector steam supply was moved to the right hand side and the pipe was extended to enter at the front end of smokebox. The whistle was moved from the cab roof on to the firebox. Manchester (London Road).

(left) The other nine were rebuilt with superheated boiler from October 1924 (6111) to April 1929 (6114) but all kept their original 19in. cylinders and slide valves. Gorton shed.

(below) Until rebuilding they had four-column Ramsbottom safety valves in rectangular casing, and a 2ft 1¼in. tall cast chimney of Robinson design.

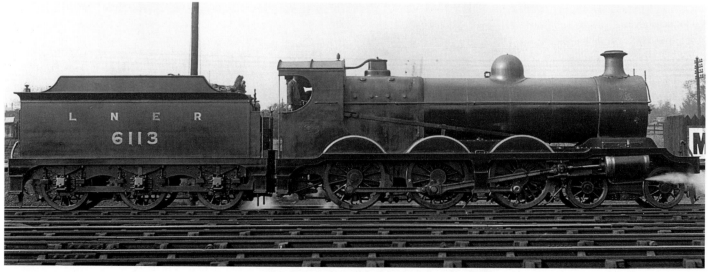

CLASS B 9

6105

Beyer, Peacock 4806.

To traffic 9/1906.

REPAIRS:
Gor. 1/1—12/8/16.**G.**
Gor. 4/12/20—6/8/21.**G.**
Gor. 14/4—23/6/23.**G.**
Gor. 23/5—15/8/25.**G.**
Gor. 30/4—27/8/27.**G.**
Superheated boiler fitted.
Gor. 5/4—17/5/30.**G.**
Gor. 25/6—9/7/32.**G.**
Gor. 24/11—8/12/34.**G.**
Gor. 14—28/11/36.**G.**
Gor. 27/8—24/9/38.**G.**
Gor. 8—22/4/39.**L.**
Gor. 7—26/7/41.**G.**
Gor. 30/10—20/11/43.**G.**
Gor. 22/6—27/7/46.**G.**
Gor. 2/4/49. *Not repaired.*

BOILERS:
1215.
1222 *(ex6111)* 12/8/16.
1176 *(new)* 6/8/21.
 830 *(new)* 27/8/27.
 641 *(ex6111)* 9/7/32.
 891 *(exQ4 6052)* 8/12/34.
1903 *(exQ4 6141)* 28/11/36.
 897 *(ex6109)* 24/9/38.
 905 *(exQ4 6134)* 26/7/41.
 640 *(exB5 5180)* 20/11/43.
3727 *(exB5 5184)* 27/7/46.

SHEDS:
Lincoln 5/19.
Gorton 8/10/25.
Trafford Park 24/11/27.
Gorton 19/3/30.
Trafford Park 4/6/30.
Gorton 30/5/32.
Trafford Park 4/3/33.
Gorton 13/7/34.
Trafford Park 17/3/37.
Gorton 5/8/38.
Trafford Park 30/9/38.
Heaton Mersey 11/10/41.
Trafford Park 22/4/45.
Heaton Mersey 6/5/45.

RENUMBERED:
6105 15/8/25.
1469 3/11/46.
61469 12/2/49.

CONDEMNED: 2/4/49.
Cut up at Dukinfield.

6106

Beyer, Peacock 4807.

To traffic 9/1906.

REPAIRS:
Gor. 19/8—7/10/11.**G.**
New R H cylinder fitted.
Gor. 17/4—5/6/20.**G.**
Gor. 18/2—29/4/22.**G.**
Gor. 5/1—29/3/24.**G.**
Gor. 26/9/25—23/1/26.**G.**
Superheated boiler fitted.
Gor. 3/3—21/4/28.**G.**
Gor. 21/6—26/7/30.**G.**
Gor. 24/9—8/10/32.**G.**
Gor. 21/10—18/11/33.**L.**
After collision.
Gor. 30/3—20/4/35.**G.**
Gor. 12—26/6/37.**G.**
Gor. 4/11—2/12/39.**G.**
Gor. 31/7—22/8/42.**G.**
Gor. 28/12/43—29/1/44.**H.**
New cylinders fitted.
Gor. 2—9/12/44.**L.**
After collision.
Gor. 9—30/3/46.**G.**
Gor. 24—31/8/46.**L.**
After collision.
Gor. 22/2—15/3/47.**L.**

BOILERS:
1216.
1224 *(ex6114)* 7/10/11.
1207 *(new)* 5/6/20.
1212 *(ex6107)* 29/3/24.
 646 *(new)* 23/1/26.
 899 *(exB5 6071)* 8/10/32.
 601 *(ex6108)* 20/4/35.
 899 *(ex6112)* 26/6/37.
 875 *(exB5 5183)* 2/12/39.
 896 *(exQ4 6133)* 22/8/42.
 838 *(exQ4 5164)* 30/3/46.

SHEDS:
Gorton 19/8/21.
Trafford Park *by* 7/6/26.
Gorton 8/8/28.
Trafford Park 27/8/28.
Gorton 4/6/30.
Trafford Park 9/9/30.
Gorton 29/8/32.
Trafford Park 27/10/32.
Gorton 11/10/33.
Trafford Park 17/6/35.
Gorton 19/1/37.
Trafford Park 13/10/37.
Gorton 27/9/39.
Trafford Park 6/4/41.

Gorton 21/9/41.
Brunswick 11/3/45.

RENUMBERED:
6106 3/5/24.
1470 16/11/46.

CONDEMNED: 19/11/48.
Into Gor. for cut up 20/11/48 but cut up at Dukinfield.

6107

Beyer, Peacock 4808.

To traffic 9/1906.

REPAIRS:
Gor. 5/5—3/7/09.**G.**
New R H cylinder fitted.
Gor. 13/7—5/10/12.**G.**
Gor. 13/4/18—30/8/19.**G.**
Awaiting new boiler.
Gor. 1/10/21—21/1/22.**G.**
Gor. 29/9—10/11/23.**G.**
Gor. 11/7—26/9/25.**G.**
Gor. 23/7—24/9/27.**G.**
Gor. 3/11/28—12/1/29.**G.**
Superheated boiler fitted.
Gor. 14/2—14/3/31.**G.**
Gor. 12/8—16/9/33.**G.**
Gor. 28/9—12/10/35.**G.**
Gor. 30/10—20/11/37.**G.**
Gor. 30/3—27/4/40.**G.**
New R H cylinder fitted.
Gor. 17/2—13/3/43.**G.**
Gor. 16/6—7/745.**G.**

BOILERS:
1217.
1219 *(ex6109)* 5/10/12.
1212 *(new)* 30/8/19.
 117 *(new)* 10/11/23.
1696 *(exQ4 5144)* 12/1/29.
1777 *(exB5 5182)* 14/3/31.
 407 *(exB5 5185)* 16/9/33.
 725 *(exB5 5187)* 12/10/35.
1920 *(exQ4 5956)* 20/11/37.
 850 *(exQ4 5049)* 27/4/40.
 899 *(exB5 5183)* 13/3/43.
 723 *(ex6112)* 7/7/45.

SHEDS:
Lincoln 19/5/22.
Gorton 20/4/25.
Trafford Park 18/3/30.
Gorton 9/9/30.
Trafford Park 6/1/32.
Gorton 14/7/33.
Trafford Park 19/6/36.

Gorton 13/10/37.
Trafford Park 6/4/41.
Gorton 21/9/41.
Heaton Mersey 8/11/41.

RENUMBERED:
1107c 24/11/23.
6107 26/9/25.
1471 17/11/46.

CONDEMNED: 20/11/47.
Cut up at Dukinfield.

6108

Beyer, Peacock 4809.

To traffic 9/1906.

REPAIRS:
Gor. 2/11/12—18/1/13.**G.**
Gor. 3/9—26/11/21.**G.**
Gor. 9/2—26/4/24.**G.**
Gor. 4/12/26—5/2/27.**G.**
Gor. 28/4—30/6/28.**G.**
Superheated boiler fitted.
Gor. 17/5—28/6/30.**G.**
Gor. 23/7—13/8/32.**G.**
Gor. 16—23/2/35.**G.**
Gor. 28/11—12/12/36.**G.**
Gor. 6—27/2/37.**L.**
L.H. cylinder broken.
Gor. 13/5—10/6/39.**G.**
Gor. 22/4—9/5/42.**G.**
Gor. 8/2—11/3/44.**G.**
Gor. 16/6/45.**L.**
Tender repair only.

BOILERS:
1218.
1217 *(ex6107)* 18/1/13.
 42 *(new)* 26/4/24.
 852 *(new)* 30/6/28.
 601 *(exQ4 6054)* 13/8/32.
 841 *(exQ4 6134)* 23/2/35.
 912 *(exQ4 5151)* 12/12/36.
 642 *(ex6110)* 10/6/39.
1903 *(ex6110)* 9/5/42.

SHEDS:
Lincoln 19/5/22.
Gorton 10/2/27.
Trafford Park 8/8/28.
Gorton 24/8/28.
Trafford Park 24/11/30.
Gorton 11/7/32.
Trafford Park 29/8/32.
Gorton 27/10/32.
Trafford Park 3/11/32.
Gorton 2/2/35.

At rebuilding the safety valves were changed to two Ross 'pops' without a casing at their base, on boilers built from 1922 onwards. The higher pitched boiler required a shorter chimney and the first used was a built-up type only 1ft 3in. tall which gave a height from rail of 12ft 7¾in. Colwick shed.

This was a boiler built in July 1920 for Q4 class and prepared with a base plate to take the Ramsbottom safety valves into which the Ross 'pops' were fitted. The 1ft 3in. built-up chimney proved too short and was superseded by a 1ft 5½in. type. This gave 12ft 10¼in. from rail still well inside the composite load gauge. Colwick shed.

In the later 1930's all had the built-up type replaced by a cast pattern 1ft 5½in. tall and more in keeping with GCR style. Trafford Park, 1939.

The first ones superheated got a new boiler and had a Gresley snifter for element protection. There were at least three where the anti-vacuum valve was fitted to the end of the header and thus protruded from the smokebox side. Annesley shed, September 1933.

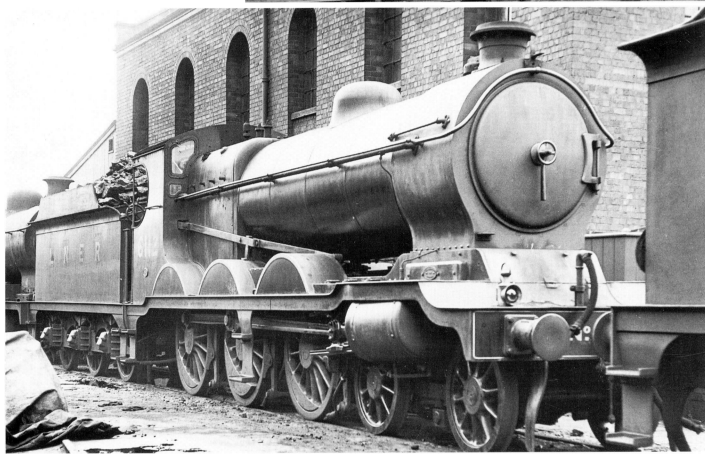

(above) All subsequently had the anti-vacuum valve in the normal position behind the chimney. Note the tender is a railed type, plated outside and was only a temporary coupling for a works visit. No.6112's tender from pre-Grouping to withdrawal had a beaded edge to the coping (see page 123). Note that the top lamp iron is now moved to the front of the smokebox.

(right) A standard fitting, until during the 1939-1945 war, was a lamp bracket on top of the smokebox, and a wheel and handle for fastening the smokebox door. Gorton shed, July 1937.

6108 continued.
Trafford Park 19/7/35.
Gorton 1/9/36.
Trafford Park 4/3/37.

RENUMBERED:
6108 26/4/24.
1472 9/11/46.

CONDEMNED: 2/6/47.
Into Gor. for cut up 7/6/47.

6109

Beyer, Peacock 4810.

To traffic 9/1906.

REPAIRS:
Gor. 23/3—15/6/12.**G.**
Gor. 30/3—26/10/18.**G.**
Gor. 19/2—2/4/21.**G.**
Gor. 30/12/22—12/5/23.**G.**
Gor. 5/7—15/11/24.**G.**
Superheated boiler & new 21in type 8K cylinders fitted.
Gor. 18/12/26—20/2/27.**G.**
Gor. 19/3—9/4/27.**L.**
Gor. 29/12/28—16/2/29.**G.**
Gor. 30/8—11/10/30.**G.**
Gor. 9—23/4/32.**G.**
Gor. 23/6—14/7/34.**G.**
Gor. 25/4—9/5/36.**G.**
Gor. 20/8—17/9/38.**G.**
Gor. 3—31/5/41.**G.**
Gor. 9—21/8/43.**G.**
Gor. 5/1—2/2/46.**G.**
Gor. 25/1—1/2/47.**L.**
Loose cylinders
Gor. 31/12/47. *Not repaired.*

BOILERS:
1219.
1216 *(ex6106)* 15/6/12.
1223 *(ex6113)* 26/10/18.
 591 *(new)* 15/11/24.
 913 *(new)* 16/2/29.
 650 *(exQ4 6133)* 23/4/32.
 849 *(exB5 5181)* 14/7/34.
 897 *(exQ4 6178)* 9/5/36.
 468 *(exQ4 5163)* 17/9/38.
 841 *(exB5 5182)* 21/8/43.
 333 *(exB5 5187)* 2/2/46.

SHEDS:
Gorton 19/8/21.
Trafford Park 15/4/29.
Gorton 25/10/29.
Trafford Park 11/7/32.
Gorton 23/3/34.
Trafford Park 21/6/41.

RENUMBERED:
6109 15/11/24.
1473 27/10/46.

CONDEMNED: 31/12/47.
Cut up at Dukinfield.

6110

Beyer, Peacock 4811.

To traffic 10/1906.

REPAIRS:
Gor. 16/8—20/9/13.**G.**
Gor. 7/6/19—17/1/20.**G.**
New L.H. cylinder fitted.
Gor. 8/4—1/7/22.**G.**
Gor. 16/2—26/4/24.**G.**
Gor. 20/2—14/8/26.**G.**
Superheated boiler fitted.
Gor. 20/4—1/6/29.**G.**
Gor. 30/1—13/2/32.**G.**
Gor. 10/2—3/3/34.**G.**
Gor. 27/6—18/7/36.**G.**
Gor. 1—29/10/38.**G.**
Gor. 2/9/39.**L.**
After collision.
Gor. 30/1—21/2/42.**G.**
Gor. 27/5—17/6/44.**G.**

BOILERS:
1220.
1218 *(ex6108)* 20/9/13.
1827 *(new)* 17/1/20.
1207 *(ex6106)* 26/4/24.
 725 *(new)* 14/8/26.
 419 *(exQ4 6139)* 13/2/32.
 642 *(exB5 6068)* 3/3/34.
1903 *(ex6105)* 29/10/38.
 852 *(exQ4 5070)* 21/2/42.
 905 *(ex6105)* 17/6/44.

SHEDS:
Gorton 19/8/21.
Trafford Park ?/?.
Gorton 15/4/29.
Trafford Park 13/8/29.
Gorton 6/1/32.
Trafford Park 30/4/32.
Gorton 3/11/32.
Trafford Park 23/3/34.
Gorton 1/4/36.
Trafford Park 27/9/39.
Gorton 21/9/41.
Trafford Park 22/3/42.

RENUMBERED:
6110 26/4/24.
1474 24/11/46.

CONDEMNED: 7/10/47.
Into Gor. for cut up 11/10/47.

6111

Beyer, Peacock 4812.

To traffic 10/1906.

REPAIRS:
Gor. 17/12/10—28/1/11.**G.**
Gor. 25/9—16/10/15.**G.**
Gor. 7/5—24/9/21.**G.**
Gor. 29/3—18/10/24.**G.**
Superheated boiler fitted.
Gor. 30/4—25/6/27.**G.**
Gor. 17/8—5/10/29.**G.**
Gor. 4—18/6/32.**G.**
Gor. 11—25/8/34.**G.**
Gor. 19/9—3/10/36.**G.**
Gor. 8—29/1/38.**L.**
After collision.
Gor. 7—21/10/39.**G.**
Gor. 2—19/12/42.**G.**
Gor. 4—11/11/44.**L.**
Gor. 18/1—29/3/47.**G.**
New cylinders fitted.

BOILERS:
1221.
1222 *(ex6112)* 28/1/11.
1220 *(ex6110)* 16/10/15.
 553 *(new)* 18/10/24.
 641 *(exQ4 5139)* 5/10/29.
 913 *(ex6109)* 18/6/32.
 830 *(exB5 6071)* 25/8/34.
 901 *(exB5 5180)* 3/10/36.
 837 *(exQ4 5151)* 21/10/39.
3738 *(new)* 19/12/42.
 896 *(ex6106)* 29/3/47.

SHEDS:
Lincoln ?/10/16.
Gorton 12/11/26.
Trafford Park 28/11/27.
Gorton 13/8/29.
Trafford Park 25/10/29.
Gorton 30/4/32.
Trafford Park 2/2/35.
Gorton 19/6/36.
Trafford Park 5/8/38.
Gorton 30/9/38.
Heaton Mersey 7/12/39.
Gorton 8/11/41.
Brunswick 9/5/43.
Heaton Mersey 18/7/43.

RENUMBERED:
 6111 18/10/24.
 1475 27/10/46.
61475 12/2/49.

WITHDRAWN: 7/7/39.
CME Order No.953 for repair issued 11/9/39.

CONDEMNED: 16/5/49.
Cut up at Dukinfield.

6112

Beyer, Peacock 4813.

To traffic 10/1906.

REPAIRS:
Gor. 19/3—23/4/10.**G.**
Gor. 31/3—29/4/11.**G.**
New L.H. cylinder fitted.
Gor. 23/11/18—25/10/19.**G.**
Gor. 21/1—8/4/22.**G.**
Gor. 23/8—20/12/24.**G.**
Superheated boiler fitted.
Gor. 9/4—28/5/27.**G.**
Gor. 15/12/28—9/2/29.**G.**
Gor. 28/2—28/3/31.**G.**
Gor. 1—22/4/33.**G.**
Gor. 15/6—6/7/35.**G.**
Heat conn. fitted at front.
Gor. 8/5—5/6/37.**G.**
Gor. 3/2—2/3/40.**G.**
New cylinders fitted.
Gor. 15/12/42—16/1/43.**G.**
Gor. 3/2—3/3/45.**G.**
Gor. 15/3—26/4/47.**G.**
Gor. 9—23/8/47.**L.**

BOILERS:
1222.
 827 *(exB5 5182)* 23/4/10.
1216 *(ex6109)* 25/10/19.
 595 *(new)* 20/12/24.
1696 *(ex6107)* 28/3/31.
1711 *(exQ4 5162)* 22/4/33.
 899 *(ex6106)* 6/7/35.
1918 *(exQ4 5958)* 5/6/37.
 910 *(exB5 6072)* 2/3/40.
 723 *(exB5 6071)* 16/1/43.
 915 *(ex6113)* 3/3/45.
3733 *(exB5 5183)* 26/4/47.

SHEDS:
Lincoln *at* 4/22.
Gorton 26/5/27.
Trafford Park 28/5/32.
Gorton 4/3/33.
Trafford Park 31/5/40.
Gorton 6/11/42.
Brunswick 27/6/43.
Gorton 31/7/43.
Trafford Park 13/8/44.

RENUMBERED:
6112 20/12/24.
1476 10/11/46

CONDEMNED: 19/8/48.
Into Gor. for cut up 21/8/48 but cut up at Dukinfield.

All had, and retained, GCR design buffers with circular head, and none acquired GS type. The front-end heater connection was only provided from about 1930 (compare with centre illustration page 116). Gorton shed.

(above) During the later part of the war, some had the top lamp bracket moved down and fixed on the smokebox door with the fastening wheel replaced by another handle. But there were exceptions (see page 122, bottom). Gorton shed.

(right) Apart from No.6110, all had the standard 4000-gallon tender with solid coping and beaded edge. No.6110 had a tender built for D9 No.6038 with open rails which were not plated behind until February 1932.

During 1923 only three got LNER - 1109 (7th July), 1105 (18th August) and 1107c (24th November). Before rebuilding began, seven acquired LNER livery but only 6110 (26th April 1924) and 6106 (3rd May 1924) combined with it the same number on a GCR style large brass plate. No.6108 got a large plate but on 26th April 1924 was sent out unpainted and did not change to LNER until 5th February 1927. Of the 1923 painted engines two, 6105 and 6107, changed to those numbers 15th August 1925 and 26th September 1925 before being rebuilt but 6109 got that number at rebuilding. Nos.6114 (30th August 1924) and 6113 (6th September 1924) [see page 116, bottom] also got LNER in original state and only on 6111 (18th October 1924) and 6112 (20th December 1924) did LNER number and rebuilding coincide.

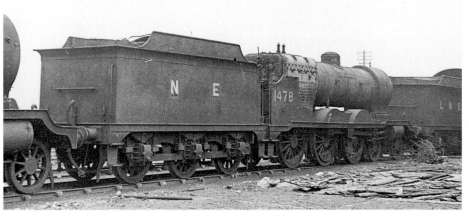

(above) From March 1929 the number was moved to cab and 12in. LNER could then be used on the tender. No.6113, on 11th April 1931, was the last B9 to get its number on the cab. Well into the 1930's this class continued to get single red lining and have polished brass beading to their splashers. By 1938/1939 most were in plain black. Trafford Park shed.

(left) Between July 1942 and January 1946 only NE was put on the tender and all ten were so treated. Although renumbered in 1946, five Nos.1471, 1472, 1474, 1477 and 1478 still had only NE on their tenders when they were withdrawn. Dukinfield works, March 1948.

LNER in shaded transfers was restored to the tenders of Nos.1469, 1470, 1473, 1475 and 1476 and they were also used for the cab numbers as late as 29th March 1947 for No.1475 (*see* page 121, centre) and 26th April 1947 for No.1476. Note the angular dome cover Gorton had adopted. Trafford Park shed, October 1947.

6113

Beyer, Peacock 4814.

To traffic 10/1906.

REPAIRS:
Gor. 21/4—2/6/17.**G.**
New R.H. cylinder fitted.
Gor. 21/8—18/9/20.**L.**
New L.H. cylinder fitted.
Gor. 6/5—15/7/22.**G.**
Gor. 12/4—16/8/24.**G.**
Gor. 22/8—12/12/25.**G.**
Superheated boiler fitted.
Gor. 15/12/28—26/1/29.**G.**
Gor. 14/3—11/4/31.**G.**
Gor. 10/6—1/7/33.**G.**
Gor. 11/1—1/2/36.**G.**
Gor. 25/9—30/10/37.**H.**
Gor. 30/12/39—20/1/40.**G.**
Gor. 12/8—20/9/41.**L.**
R.H. cylinder loose.
Gor. 31/10—21/11/42.**G.**
Gor. 19—29/1/44.**L.**
Gor. 29/7—26/8/44.**G.**
Gor. 25/8/47. *Not repaired.*

BOILERS:
1223.
1215 *(ex6105)* 2/6/17.
1223 *(ex6109)* 16/8/24.
643 *(new)* 12/12/25.
1912 *(exQ4 5959)* 11/4/31.
1696 *(ex6112)* 1/7/33.
3722 *(new)* 1/2/36.
901 *(ex6111)* 20/1/40.
915 *(?/?)* 21/11/42.
525 *(exB5 5186)* 26/8/44.

SHEDS:
Gorton 19/8/21.
Trafford Park 14/7/33.
Gorton 19/7/35.
Trafford Park 31/3/36.
Gorton 4/3/37.
Trafford Park 13/4/40.

RENUMBERED:
6113 6/9/24.
1477 9/11/46.

CONDEMNED: 25/8/47.
Cut up at Gorton.

6114

Beyer, Peacock 4815.

To traffic 10/1906.

REPAIRS:
Gor. 28/4--27/5/11.**G.**
Gor. 26/11/21—25/3/22.**G.**
Gor. 8/3—16/8/24.**G.**
Gor. 6/2—3/4/26.**G.**
Gor. 13/8—12/11/27.**G.**
Gor. 9/2—27/4/29.**G.**
Superheated boiler fitted.
Gor. 24/1—21/2/31.**G.**
Gor. 25/3—8/4/33.**G.**
Gor. 27/7—17/8/35.**G.**
Gor. 19/6—17/7/37.**G.**
Gor. 6—27/1/40.**G.**
Gor. 2—26/12/42.**G.**
Gor. 30/6—28/7/45.**G.**
Gor. 27/4—25/5/46.**L.**
New cylinders fitted.

BOILERS:
1224.
1221 *(ex6111)* 27/5/11.
1827 *(ex6110)* 16/8/24.
1772 *(exB5 6067)* 27/4/29.
728 *(exB5 5180)* 8/4/33.

920 *(exQ4 5092)* 17/8/35.
650 *(exB5 6077)* 17/7/37.
3722 *(ex6113)* 27/1/40.
901 *(exB5 6072)* 28/7/45.

SHEDS:
Gorton 10/2/20.
Trafford Park 18/7/34.
Gorton 17/6/35.
Trafford Park 13/4/40.
Gorton 6/11/42.
Brunswick 26/8/45.

RENUMBERED:
6114 30/8/24.
1478 25/8/46

CONDEMNED: 10/12/47.
*Into Gor. for cut up 13/12/47
but cut up at Dukinfield.*

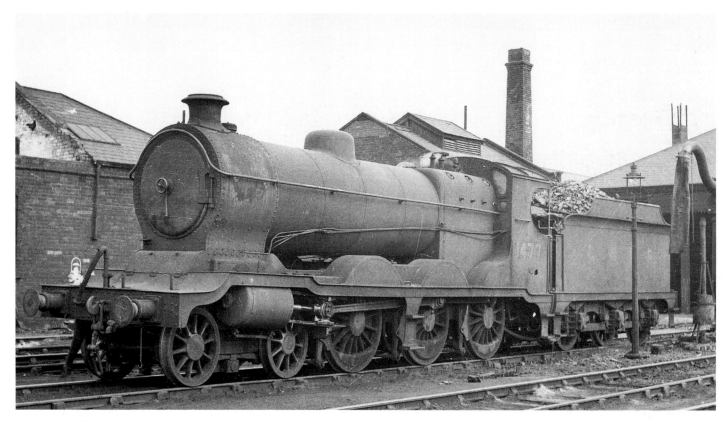

From April 1947 No.1477 ran with the tender from 1473 which had LNER restored. This was a straight exchange as 1473 then ran to withdrawal with only NE on its tender. No.1477 (as 6113) was the last at Gorton for repair on 26th August 1944 and so retained the lamp iron on top of the smokebox and the wheel on the smokebox door to withdrawal on 25th August 1947. Trafford Park shed, April 1947.

To avoid any confusion with LM Region engines also at Stockport (Heaton Mersey) shed, the two B9 there were put into their British Railways numbers 61469 on 12th February 1949 and 61475 on the same date. Correct Gill sans 10in. figures were painted on but LNER on the tender was not changed. Heaton Mersey shed, March 1949.

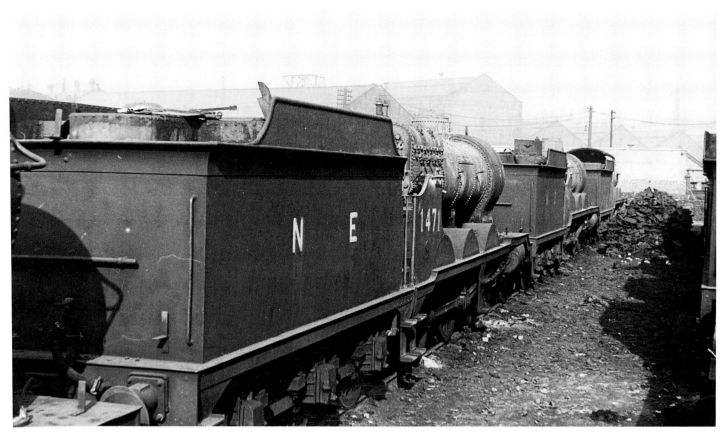

Between 25th August and 24th November 1946 all ten had their number changed to 1469, 1470, 1471, 1472, 1473, 1474, 1475, 1476, 1477 and 1478 but only four survived for British Railways to take over on 1st January 1948. No.1471 was withdrawn on 20th November 1947 and only this progress had been made in cutting up the engine by 12th March 1948. The tender was sold for scrapping in May 1948. Gorton works.

No.1475 got new cylinders at a general repair, ex works as late as 29th March 1947. From that 18th January to 29th March 1947 general repair, here on 14th April 1947, No.1475 is at Manchester (Central) station loco yard and is still probably doing trial trips from Gorton shed before release to its home shed of Heaton Mersey.

Immingham shed circa 1920 and Gorton based No.1113 is ready for its return working to Manchester.

Tenderless but otherwise intact, 61475 awaits its fate at Dukinfield works in June 1949.